ALFRED THE GREAT

ALFRED THE GREAT

P. J. HELM

"... to shew the latitude of the King's
Mind and Genius, in all Dimensions truly
Royal and August ..."
Sir John Spelman, 1643

BARNES
&NOBLE
BOOKS
NEW YORK

To

Francis John Wiley

Copyright © 1963 by P. J. Helm
All rights reserved.

This edition published by Barnes & Noble, Inc.,
by arrangement with HarperCollins Publishers, Inc.

1995 Barnes & Noble Books

ISBN 1-56619-652-3

Printed and bound in the United States of America

M 9 8 7 6 5 4 3 2 1

Contents

Acknowledgements

The author wishes to thank the following for permission to quote from their works—George Allen and Unwin Ltd.: Russell, *History of Western Philosophy*; Cambridge University Press: P. Hunter Blair, *An Introduction to Anglo-Saxon England*; The Clarendon Press: Stenton, *Anglo-Saxon England* and Hodgkin, *History of the Anglo-Saxons*, Vol. II; Constable and Company Ltd.: Robin Flower, "Pangur Ban" from *Poems and Translations*, and Helen Waddell, *Medieval Latin Lyrics*; J. M. Dent and Sons Ltd.: R. K. Gordon, *Anglo-Saxon Poetry*; Eyre and Spottiswoode (Publishers) Ltd.: Dorothy Whitelock's edition of *The Anglo-Saxon Chronicle*; and Penguin Books Ltd.: D. Wright's translation of *Beowulf*.

ENGLAND at the time of Alfred's death

~~ Boundary laid down in the Treaty of ALFRED & GUTHRUM

NORTHUMBRIA

KINGDOM OF YORK

York

DANELAW

Chester

DANISH

Torksey

Nottingham

WALES

OFFA'S DYKE

WATLING STREET

Buttington

Repton

MERCIA

Crowland

EAST ANGLIA

SAXON MERCIA

Hoxne

Cambridge

Gloucester

Wantage

London

Benfleet

Shoeburyness

Cheddar

Chippenham

Ashdown

Reading

Thanet

Milton

Cynuit

Edington

Wedmore

Farnham

KENT

Athelney

WESSEX

Salisbury

Winchester

Appledore

Sherborne

Exeter

Dorchester

Wareham

Quentavic

Alfred "the Great"?

So the pieces we have being mangled, and wanting the
Joints and Edges wherewith they should agree among
themselves, they seem rather the Rubbish of a Broken
Statue, than the whole Parts of a Perfect Image.
Sir John Spelman, 1643

ONLY one king of England has the title of "the Great", and
that one lived over a thousand years ago. Everyone has heard
of King Alfred, yet the ordinary person might be hard put to it to
justify the king's claim to this unique honour.

Alfred beat the Danes? He saved his own kingdom of Wessex
from being over-run, but he did not drive the invaders from the
land. On the contrary, Alfred and the Danes partitioned the
country between them, and within a hundred years or so of his
death England had become part of the Danish sea empire of
Canute.

The king founded the British Navy? There are half a dozen
candidates for that honour, and Henry VII has probably the best
claim.

Alfred ordered the White Horse to be cut on the slopes of
Salisbury Plain? That particular White Horse had certainly been
there for a thousand years already when Alfred was born.

At all events, he burnt the cakes! Maybe. . . .

There is undeniably a certain ambiguity about the popular
picture of King Alfred. That burning of the cakes is an unheroic,
almost slapstick story, something out of pantomime. Small boys
confuse King Alfred with King Arthur. He lies, too, under the
disadvantage of being what one might call an honorary Eminent
Victorian. The nineteenth century saw Alfred as a national hero,
but their view of heroism is stained for us with an unfortunate
glaze of sentimentality. The Victorians were accustomed to refer
to the king as "England's Darling". The term has a respectable

Saxon ancestry, but it is not—to a twentieth-century mind—quite the most suitable name for a Saxon chieftain.

There is an atrociously idealized picture of "Alfred and his Mother", by the nineteenth-century painter Alfred Stevens, in the National Gallery. Pale and refined, the mother leans forward and envelops the clean little boy and the immense book that he is reading. It might be Little Lord Fauntleroy and Queen Victoria.

Every generation needs to have its history, its heroes, examined afresh. It is time to replace the Victorian Alfred whose faint image —in spite of twentieth-century work—still lingers on the non-professional retina. It is the purpose of this book to describe the life and times of a Saxon king called Alfred, and to explore his right to the proud title of "the Great".

On what does the extraordinary prestige of this man, who moved on the edge of civilization over a thousand years ago, rest? Geoffrey Gaimar, an Anglo-Norman poet-chronicler of the twelfth century, wrote:

> He reigned well for twenty and eight years; there are few such men living: for he was wise and a good warrior; he knew well how to curb his enemies; there was not a better scholar than he, for he had learned in his infancy. He caused an English book to be written of deeds, and laws, of battles in the land, and of the kings who made war; and he caused many books to be written, which the learned men often went to read. May God and the kind lady Saint Mary have mercy on his soul!

This was the sort of information, most of it true but some parts a little distorted, that was available to an educated man, two hundred and fifty years after Alfred's death. That is one point of departure.

Another jumping-off point lies in Berkshire.

The village of Wantage (population 3,424) is situated where the bare Berkshire Downs sink into the Vale of the White Horse. To-day it is on the main road from Reading to Gloucester; in the ninth century it lay on one of the main roads of those days, the Icknield Way that ran diagonally across England, just above the damp, forested Lowlands, from the Wash to the Upper Thames. Grass-grown or lost today, it was a trunk route for over two thousand years.

King Alfred was born at Wantage in 849. There is a statue at the top of the High Street, where it widens out into a pleasant market square, to commemorate the fact. It is the work of Count Gleichen (1833–91). The count's full name was Prince Victor Ferdinand Franz Eugen Gustav Adolf Constantin Friedrich of Hohenlohe-Langenburg, and he was a member of the Royal Institute of Water-Colour Painters. His mother was half-sister to Queen Victoria and the count had entered the British Navy, serving with distinction in the Crimean and Second Opium Wars. Then his health had broken down. With remarkable adaptability, he set to work to make a career as an artist and sculptor. He was so successful that, when he lost his fortune in a bank failure, he was able to earn a living and even to purchase "a small house near Ascot". In 1887 the queen created him an Admiral on the retired list.

Disraeli and Salisbury sat to him, but the main work of Count Gleichen is the white figure of King Alfred at Wantage. It is not a very good statue. The king stands there, stiff and uncomfortable on his little rock, a scroll in his left hand, his right resting gently on the head of an axe. It might as well be an umbrella.

At the base of this dull respectable effort there is an inscription. One almost expects to find that the man had endowed a local Mechanics' Institute:

Alfred the Great
The West Saxon King
Born at Wantage, A.D. 849.
This statue,
The Work of H.S.H. Count Gleichen,
Was presented to the town of Wantage
By Colonel R. Lloyd Lindsay, VC., MP. for Berkshire
and was unveiled by
T.R.H. the Prince and Princess of Wales,
July 14th 1877

Alfred found learning dead,
and he restored it.
Education neglected
and he revived it.

The laws powerless,
    and he gave them force.
The Church debased,
    and he raised it.
The land ravaged by a fearful enemy,
    from which he delivered it.
Alfred's name will live as long
    as mankind shall respect the past.

Are these claims, and the words of Geoffrey Gaimar written centuries earlier, justified? Who was this man, and what did he do? What was his world like?

A Small World

Our ancestors divided all Middle-Earth, which is surrounded by the Ocean, into three parts, and called them
Asia, and Europe, and Africa, though some men have said
that there were only two parts; Asia and Europe.
King Alfred's translation of the History of Orosius

THE ninth-century European had a shadowy knowledge,
streaked with legend, of parts of Asia and Africa, but for him
civilization lay on an axis that ran from Constantinople, through
Rome, to Paris. As one moved away from that axis to the north
and west, the thin veneer of Roman ways and Christian beliefs
rapidly gave place to heathen customs and pagan superstition.
Alfred's England lay within—but only just within—the outer
fringe of this zone of civilization.

At the time of Alfred's birth Europe was moving out of a brief
period of relative peace and into one of anarchy, that was to cul-
minate in the dark tenth century. Though this movement was not,
of course, so apparent then as it is to the hindsight of the historian,
nevertheless the more far-sighted men were already conscious of
the need to save something from a civilization that was disintegrating. It is a constant theme in Alfred's writings.

Fifty years before his birth, in the year 800, Europe was clearly
divided into two parts, "Christendom" and "Heathenesse". East
of the Elbe, east of a line from modern Hamburg to Istanbul, lay
the area controlled by barbarians from the northern forests or
from Asia, men who had never been educated by the Roman
Empire or softened in their behaviour by the Christian Church.
These men, Bulgars and Magyars, Slavs and Norsemen, controlled territories the area of which shifted from decade to decade,
but always threatened the civilized world.

In the year 800 these barbarians were still contained, were even
being pushed back in places. And one knew what to think of

them; as the "Song of Roland" succinctly put it, "Christians are right, and pagans are wrong".

Four great powers shared the civilized south and west of Europe. The Byzantine Empire, the heir of the former Roman Empire, was based on Constantinople and controlled the foot of Italy, Sicily, the southern Balkans, and Asia Minor. It was old and rich, but all its energies were devoted to holding back the barbarous Serbs and Bulgars on its northern frontier, and the infidel Arabs on its southern one. It had diplomatic and economic contacts with the west, but differences of language (the polite language of the west was Latin, but the Byzantine Empire used Greek) and religious disagreement (the Roman Pope and the Orthodox Patriarch were not on speaking terms) kept it relatively isolated.

To the eyes of western visitors the Byzantine Empire was impressive for its richness and its strangeness. The greatest church in Christendom, Santa Sophia, the church of the Holy Wisdom, dominated Constantinople. "You would think," wrote an enthusiastic Byzantine, "that the building was not lighted by the sun, but that the light was produced within, such an abundance of light is poured into this church. Who would not marvel at the green colour of some stones, the purple of others, the flaming red and the blinding white. It is uniquely full of light and sunshine."

But if Santa Sophia was the greatest, it was not the most powerful church. Across the Adriatic in Italy was the Bishop of Rome, the Pope. His authority, though spiritual, was the second great force in Europe. He had always been the greatest bishop in the west, and when, four hundred years earlier, the Roman Empire collapsed, the Pope remained as a symbol of law and order, an arbiter between rival bishops or contending barbarians.

By the year 800 the Pope's spiritual power as head of the Christian church was not disputed in the west. His actual power depended on his character—and on that of his neighbours. Only a year before, in 799, Pope Leo III had been ambushed by his enemies as he was leaving his Lateran palace in Rome on the day of the Greater Litanies. They dragged him from his horse and tried, unsuccessfully, to cut out his tongue and put out his eyes. He was rescued in the nick of time, bleeding and badly injured, and managed to escape to the hill-town of Spoleto. From there he appealed for help to the third of the great European powers, Charles the Great, "Charlemagne", king of the Franks.

These Franks were former barbarians who had settled in northern France and then conquered the lands to the south. Theirs was the most powerful and civilized of the states that had grown up amid the wreckage of the Roman Empire in the west.

Recently the Frankish kings had adopted the role of protector of the Papacy. Charles's father had come to the rescue of one Pope. Charles himself had been recognized by another, twenty-five years earlier, as overlord of all Italy to the north of Naples.

Now Charles restored the mutilated Pope Leo III to Rome. In return, on Christmas Day 800, as Charles knelt at Mass in the old church of St. Peter's, Leo crowned him with a golden crown. There is a contemporary description of the event:

> Pope Leo placed a crown upon his head, and all the Roman people cried aloud: "To Charles, Augustus, crowned of God, great and pacific Emperor of the Romans, life and victory!" After the applause he was adored by the Pope after the manner of the princes of old, and, instead of Patrician, he was called Emperor and Augustus.

So Charles became an emperor; and historians have ever since been arguing about the exact significance of the dramatic scene.

Whatever lay behind it, Charles' coronation was certainly the outward and visible sign of his power. His lands stretched from beyond the Elbe south into modern Yugoslavia as far as Split. Everything to the west of that line was his, except for the greater part of Spain and the Byzantine toe of Italy. Bavaria had been annexed, the Saxons in the north had been hammered into submission in three successive campaigns, a Frankish army had crossed the Pyrenees and driven the Arab conquerors of Spain back beyond Barcelona.

All this may seem a far cry from Alfred, not yet born, but there are a great many parallels between the two men's lives. Like Alfred, Charles was not only a man of war. Throughout his huge empire—the greatest since the Romans, it was really too big—he preserved a law and order unusual for those days. The emperor codified the differing laws of his subjects—Italian Lombards, quick Gascons, his stolid native Franks. He imposed a uniform system of local government, dividing his lands into easily administered areas, called counties because they were under a count. Royal officials, the *missi dominici*, were sent direct from the emperor's court and served as a kind of royal inspectorate. They rode fast and far through the countryside, carrying even-handed justice, for Charles' orders were "they are not to be hindered in the doing of justice by the flattery or bribery of anyone, by their partiality for their own friends or by the fear of powerful men". This was something new for those days. Never since Roman times had men known such peace and security.

Charles encouraged learning and culture. A palace school was set up and the emperor insisted that the children of his nobles and officials should attend it. At court he and his scholars and his ministers formed a close circle, something between a club and a study group. Each was known by a Biblical nickname; Charles himself was King David. There, tired after hunting, they would sit and eat by torchlight, Charles himself handing out huge helpings, and listen to the scholars and the poets.

The greatest of these scholars was a foreigner, Alcuin, who had come from Yorkshire. There were others from Italy and Spain, and there were, naturally, Franks as well. One of these, Einhard, wrote a life of Charles. "Charles," he said, "was broad and strong and tall (his height seven times the length of his foot); his head round, his eyes large and lively, with a long nose, fair hair, and a laughing face." Einhard goes on to say that he was always dignified "even though his neck was thick and short, and his belly rather prominent"! He records that the emperor tried to learn to write, and kept blank tablets under his pillow which he used to practise on when he could not sleep. But his efforts "met with ill success".

All books were handwritten, of course, and the script in use had gradually degenerated into an almost illegible running hand, known as "cursive". Charles ordered a new script to be designed. The work was carried out by Alcuin. The new small-letter script —minuscule—was beautifully proportioned and easy to read, with the result that it has possessed the most remarkable life and power. It was adopted by the Italian printers of the fifteenth century as the basis for their founts of type, and has survived to the present day with very little change. This book is printed in

characters based on those worked out over a thousand years ago
at the command of an illiterate emperor.

The new script and the new learning that Charles encouraged
were used to produce what was—for the times—a flood of books:
commentaries, textbooks, histories, and at least one encyclo-
pedia. Poems were written, usually academic exercises of the
crossword puzzle type, acrostics and so on, but just occasionally
speaking from another civilization directly to us. Here is part of
the dedication of a book on gardening, addressed to an abbot-
schoolmaster:

> So might you sit in the small garden close
> In the green darkness of the apple trees
> Just where the pear tree casts its broken shade,
> And they would gather you the shining fruit
> With the soft down upon it; all your boys,
> Your little laughing boys, your happy school,
> And bring huge apples clasped in their two hands.[1]

Men trained at the palace school became bishops, set up schools
in the provinces, and other abbots and bishops in turn followed
their example. The ripples of this learning lapped against Alfred's
own court later in the century.

Charles the Great died in 814, a generation before the birth of
Alfred. Almost at once the emperor became a legendary figure.
Within a hundred years the first drafts of the "Song of Roland"
were being composed. The Song describes how Charles' best-
loved noble, Roland, is betrayed to the Spanish Arabs and dies
with the Emperor's rearguard in the Pass of Roncesvalles in the
Spanish Pyrenees. Today a narrow gap in the mountain skyline is
still known as "la brêche de Roland"—the gap cut by Roland's
sword. At the other extreme of sophistication, the figure of
Charles stands on the roof of sixteenth-century Montacute House
in Somerset. He is there as one of the Nine Worthies of Christendom in the company of Caesar and King Arthur, Joshua, David,
Judas Maccabaeus, Hector, Alexander, and Godfrey of Bouillon.

Such a reputation powerfully influenced Alfred, who could
speak with men whose fathers had known "Charlemagne",
Charles the Great.

[1] H. Waddell: *Medieval Latin Lyrics.*

The fourth great power in Europe was that of Charles' enemies, the Arabs. They had poured westwards out of the desert two hundred years before. They had seized the Near East, the North African coast and Spain. Within a hundred years of the initial outburst they were halfway across France, hammering at the gates of Tours. And Tours is only 300 miles from the English Channel.

But there they were checked by Charles the Great's grandfather, Charles Martel, in a battle near Poitiers and by the middle of the eighth century they had been rolled back beyond the Pyrenees.

Such successes were unusual however. Throughout the ninth century the Arabs remained a great power and a great menace. They controlled the southern coast of the Mediterranean and from little ports up and down that coast their light raiding ships came out and made increasingly hazardous the European trade routes to the east. At the same time Arab expeditions were constantly trying to establish a foothold on the European side of the great sea, in Sicily and on the south coast of France.

The Arabs were a threat to European civilization, but they were also a great civilization in their own right. These were the days of the splendid Caliph of the Arabian Nights, Harun-ar-Rashid of Baghdad. In Alexandria and Spanish Cordova and Seville, there were lesser Baghdads, clean, wealthy and cultured, in contact with the luxury trade from Asia.

At this time Greek scientific and philosophical writings, almost lost to the west, were being translated into Arabic. It was from these Arabic versions that western Europe later recovered many classical texts that would otherwise have been lost for ever. The Arabs were great mathematicians—the word *algebra* is derived from the Arabic. They were chemists—the word *alchemy* is Arabic too. In comparison with western Europe the Arabic science that was most advanced was that of medicine. The best textbook on eye diseases, unsurpassed till the eighteenth century, was written in the Arab city of Mosul about this time.

This then was the Europe of 800; a relatively peaceful continent dominated by the Arab Caliphates of Spain and the southern Mediterranean, the land empire of Charles the Great, the spiritual power of the Papacy, and the long-established East Roman Byzantine Empire.

Fifty years later, at the time of Alfred's birth all seemed lost. To an impartial observer it must have appeared very likely that European civilization would go under before the attacks of the barbarian and the infidel just as that of the old Roman Empire had done exactly four hundred years earlier. That it did not do so was due to many factors, and not least to the resistance of such men as Alfred.

Meanwhile the over-large empire of the Emperor Charles the Great had broken up into three parts: the West Frankish Kingdom (the western part of modern France); the East Frankish Kingdom (West Germany, Holland and Belgium, eastern France, Switzerland and Charles the Great's Italian lands); and sandwiched between these two giants, the Kingdom of Burgundy (west Switzerland, and France east of the Rhône).

The Emperor's descendants—men with names like Charles the Bald, Louis the Stammerer and Charles the Fat—wasted their strength in fratricidal strife. As they grew weaker, the local barons grew more powerful. There followed endless private wars between the ambitious particles into which the great empire had dissolved. A contemporary poet lamented: "Once we had a king, now we have kinglets. Once there was an empire, now there are fragments calling themselves kingdoms." Another Frank wrote: "Then there was everywhere abundance and happiness, now there is only poverty and misery."

The Papacy too lost both its spiritual and its political power after the days of Nicholas I (858–67). He, men said, "tamed kings and tyrants and ruled the world like a sovereign", but his successors were puppets of the Roman nobility, their pontificates stained by private feuds of Italian intensity.

In 896, for instance, Pope Stephen III presided at the trial of his predecessor, Formosus. The late Pope's body was taken from the grave in which it had been lying for eight months. The corpse was then dressed in its former vestments and wedged roughly into the throne on which their owner had once sat. A formal trial of the grisly object then took place. The corpse, not surprisingly, kept silence and was duly condemned. The robes were ripped from the body. Three fingers were chopped off—the three which had once dared to give the Papal blessing—and the mutilated corpse was tumbled into the Tiber. . . .

Beyond Rome lay the new Rome, Constantinople, but there too the heart of power had rotted. The emperor, Michael III (842–67), nicknamed "the drunkard", was famed chiefly for his success as a chariot racer.

Just at the time when Alfred's Europe lacked the leaders it so sorely needed, it began to suffer increasingly severe attacks on all fronts from its enemies.

The Arabs captured Sicily and crossed the Straits of Messina into southern Italy. In the west they moved from Spain into Provence, seized the town of Fréjus, and used it as a base from which to conduct raids into the interior.

While the Arabs swarmed across the southern sea, the Vikings from Scandinavia sailed their long boats across the northern one and plundered the shores of the British Isles and of France. From Russia to Spain they sailed up the broad rivers of western Europe, their dragon prows suddenly appearing before quiet inland towns and lonely monasteries.

Europe was not only under attack by water. From the middle of the ninth century onwards, the tribes beyond that imaginary line from the Elbe to Constantinople, that bounded the civilized world, were once more on the move. Their attacks, launched mainly against the Byzantine Empire, continued throughout the tenth century, but at the same time there were hints of a new threat to the west. From Asia little men on horseback, the Magyars, armed with light bows and arrows, ferocious fighters, made their appearance on the plains of central Europe.

One chronicler after another tells the same melancholy tale. Before the death of Alfred, the Magyar ponies had cantered into north Italy, Provence and Lorraine.

> "The Vikings ravaged all the land on both banks of the Seine." . . . "The cities are empty, the monasteries burned, the country a desert". . . . "The Saracens slaughtered all the Christians whom they found outside the walls of Rome". . . . "Men devour one another like the fishes of the sea. . . ."

Everywhere the prayers of the weak and the smoke of burning buildings mingled in the air. It was a hundred and fifty years before a stable pattern emerged.

In each country men had to hammer out their own solution to the problems the new threats posed. The British Isles were not isolated from these dangers. The Channel was not a barrier, but a link with Europe. The North Sea was the Vikings' home. England was more caught up in European affairs at the time of Alfred's birth than in many later centuries.

The islands were not a unit. In the north and west lived the British, to the south and east the English. This division was the consequence of a fundamental difference between the two areas—a difference still apparent today beneath the surface of twentieth-century unity.

Drive north or west out of London. The land is low-lying, flat or gently rolling, agriculturally valuable. The villages are tight little knots, miniature towns, often with a green, or an open space of some sort in the centre.

But drive on far enough and eventually, in whichever direction you travel, the character of the countryside changes. The hills get higher, the valleys narrower. The agriculture becomes rougher and, most obvious of all, villages give place to scattered little hamlets. Fences are supplemented by stone walls, thatch and tiles by slates.

These in general are the sort of differences between highland and lowland Britain—between, roughly, land over 600 ft. and land lying at a lower level. It is not only a question of height above sea-level, though. In the south and east the soil is often clay, hard to work, but rich when once the forests which grow there have been cleared. What hills there are consist of chalk or limestone, bare and well-drained. The rainfall is low. To the north and west the soils tend to be poorer, and the land is much wetter as the great rains drive in from the Atlantic.

Of course, there is no clear-cut boundary between these two regions, one moves imperceptibly from one to the other. Imagine, however, a line drawn from York to Exeter—the highland zone lies to the north and west of that line.

The fertile, open lowland lies conveniently on the European side of Britain. Convenient, that is, for traders and invaders. Again and again until the Norman Conquest invaders made the narrow Channel crossing and rolled the previous inhabitants back into the less attractive, but more easily defended, highland zone. This was, in fact, how Alfred's Saxon ancestors had established themselves. They had come to Britain after the collapse of the Roman government here, about four centuries before Alfred's birth.

As Alfred's biographer, Sir John Spelman, wrote in the seventeenth century

> ... the *Britains* were to a very small part cut off and chased from their Native Soil, and the residue being driven into a Corner were not otherwise secure there, than by the wild and mountainous site thereof, and the best of their country possess'd by Enemies even before their Eyes.

By Alfred's time all this was ancient history. He was parted from the original invaders by as great a stretch of time as separates us from Queen Elizabeth I. Britain—or at least the lowland zone —was now the Saxon homeland, England. Originally pagan, the Saxons had now been Christians for two hundred years and their little kingdoms were an integral part of European civilization.

But in the north and west British chiefs and the British way of life survived. Scotland was controlled by the Picts, the "tattooed men", and the Scots (who had come from Ireland). The boundary between the Scots and the English did not lie east and west as it does today but ran north and south along the Pennines. To the west of the mountains the Scottish kingdom of Strathclyde included not only the south-west of Scotland but also the whole of the Lake District, while to the east the Saxons held the coast right up to the Firth of Forth. There a Saxon king of the seventh century had established his burh and called it "Edwin's fortress"— Edinburgh.

Wales, known then as "North Wales", was an independent kingdom, or collection of kingdoms, as local wars dictated. Its eastern boundary ran in the same general direction as it does today, from Cheshire to Chepstow. A hundred years earlier the Saxon king Offa had ordered the construction of a great earthwork stretching for more than a hundred miles to mark the boundary between the Welsh cattle-raiders—for "Taffy was a Welshman, Taffy was a thief"—and the Saxon farmers. The bracken-covered hump of Offa's Dyke can still be seen in many places, rising unexpectedly out of green fields like the back of some great fish.

To the south, across the Bristol Channel, there had once existed the kingdom of "West Wales", Cornwall; but that land had been finally conquered only twenty years before Alfred's birth.

Across the Irish Sea lay the kingdom of Ireland, ruled by a High King and four fellow kings with power in their respective territories of Ulster, Meath, Leinster, Munster and Connaught—a system that made for disunity and played into the hands of the local chieftains. Yet learning and the arts flourished, at least in the monasteries. One remembers the lovely honey-coloured crosses at Clonmacnois, the Book of Kells with its intricately illuminated initials, the Irish monks carrying Christianity north to Scotland, south to Lombardy. In Alfred's day the greatest scholar at the Frankish court was an Irishman, John "the Scot". A fellow countryman in the monastery at Reichenau on the shores of Lake Constance, wrote the following poem:

> I and Pangur Ban my cat,
> 'Tis a like task we are at;
> Hunting mice is his delight,
> Hunting words I sit all night.
>
> 'Tis a merry thing to see
> At our tasks how glad are we,
> When at home we sit and find
> Entertainment to our mind.
>
> 'Gainst the wall he sets his eye,
> Full and fierce and sharp and sly;
> 'Gainst the wall of knowledge I
> All my little wisdom try.
>
> So in peace our task we ply,
> Pangur Ban, my cat, and I;
> In our arts we find our bliss,
> I have mine and he has his.

That is a witty poem, and the man who wrote it must have had an urbane mind. It would be a mistake to write off the British states as the homes of barbarous highlanders and narrow hermits.

Nevertheless the greatest wealth, the strongest links with Europe, the most advanced political machinery in Britain were all to be found in the lowland Saxon kingdoms. At first the Saxons had come in groups, little isolated tribal families, but these had soon coalesced or been swallowed up by their neighbours until, two hundred years after the original invasions, seven kingdoms shared the land: Northumbria, Mercia, East Anglia, Essex, Kent, Sussex and Wessex. Three of these in turn stood head and shoulders above the rest.

In the north-east was Northumbria, stretching from Edinburgh to the Humber. Its golden age had been in the middle of the seventh century. Then its monasteries at Lindisfarne and Jarrow had been centres of learning, and its kings had almost succeeded in uniting Saxon England under one rule. Their overlordship extended from the Scottish lowlands to the Isle of Wight.

The power of Northumbria collapsed with dramatic suddenness. It is not difficult to see why. The kingdom lay too far from the centre of things, its link with Europe confined to one small lifeline, the ancestor of the Great North Road. It was thinly peopled. Most important of all, the members of its ruling house destroyed one another in blood feuds of an almost Sicilian ferocity. Of fourteen kings in the eighth century, five were murdered and four more deposed or forced to abdicate!

To the south of Northumbria lay the kingdom of Mercia, occupying the midlands. It took its name from the "marches" or frontiers which it held against the wild Welsh. After the decline of Northumbria, the kings of Mercia were the next rulers to make a bid for the control of all England.

Under Offa (757–96) the bid almost succeeded. The king took the title of *Rex Anglorum*, King of the English, and he was at least nominally overlord of all Britain south of the Humber. Offa's Dyke still demonstrates the power at his command. He was connected by marriage with the emperor, Charles the Great. Offa minted a gold coinage, in those days a sign of great economic stability. (It was copied from an Arabic gold dinar and the copyist thought the Arab script was only fancy scroll-work. So Christian Offa's coins circulated with the proud inscription in Arabic: "There is no God but one, and Mahomet is his Prophet"!)

Yet when Offa died his kingdom broke up again into its component parts, of which the greatest was Wessex.

Northumbria and Mercia had in turn achieved, but failed to keep, the overlordship of England. Last came the chance of the royal house of Wessex. Its kings succeeded, against all the balance of probability—for the two northern kingdoms had bulked larger than Wessex in the past.

The kingdom of Wessex had been founded by Saxon invaders pressing up the Thames valley. Originally it included neither London, already the main commercial doorway to the island, nor Canterbury, the spiritual capital. About the year 800, its lands lay in Hampshire, Wiltshire, Dorset, Somerset, Devon, and the half-conquered "West Wales". It was not an impressive heritage.

Why then did Wessex succeed when Northumbria—first in the field—and Mercia—at first sight apparently more suitably placed—failed?

The kingdom had certain advantages. Its boundaries were "natural" ones: the Bristol Channel and the English Channel, and the Thames valley to the north. Mercia had lacked these, except to the west. The kings of Mercia had no sort of capital either. They moved from Tamworth to Repton, from Repton to Lichfield. The rulers of Wessex built up Winchester into a centre with something of the status of a royal city. They made some effort, too, to assimilate the original British inhabitants. The laws of Ine, king of Wessex from 688 to 725, had given the conquered Britons a definite niche in the social structure. True they were only assessed at half the value of an Englishman, but they had their legally defined and protected rights. They appear in the king's service and even in the charmed circle of the king's personal guard. This tolerant attitude towards "the natives" must have given these western lands an increased social stability. Wessex was, too, always prepared to treat the British kings of Wales as equals and to make alliances with them.

Another factor, perhaps, in the strength of Wessex was that it lay along the Channel and was therefore peculiarly well-placed to receive stimuli from the charged points of civilization on the continent. There was of course another side to this proximity. The kingdom was equally well-placed to receive the attention of invaders and of raiders, sailing direct to England or turning back empty-handed from the Frankish coast. Here there was great danger, but the danger might prove a spur to action—if it could be resisted. Wessex would be kept, as it were, on its toes by the stimulus of pressure. Everything depended on whether or not the rulers of Wessex could rise to the challenge of their environment.

What picture did the Saxons have of these islands? Almost a hundred years before Alfred's birth Bede, living at the wind-swept monastery of Jarrow in Northumbria, finished the first history of Britain. The island, he says, is 800 miles long and 200 wide, and the coastline measures 3,675 miles. From the nearest part of the continent you can see Richborough in Kent; from there to Boulogne is about fifty miles. North of Britain lie the Orkneys. The nights are very long in winter, lasting eighteen hours, but are correspondingly short in summer. There is good pasture, plenty of grain and timber and vineyards. There are salmon and eel fisheries, dolphins, seals and sometimes whales. Shellfish are plentiful and are useful as a source of dyes. Bede is especially enthusiastic about the cockles—"a beautiful scarlet dye is extracted from them which remains unfaded by sunshine or rain". Natural springs provide hot baths, and there are veins of iron, lead, copper and silver. There is also jet—when it is rubbed, things will cling to it, as they do to amber, and when it is burned it drives away snakes.

A brief, but on the whole an accurate, account.

The Youngest Son (849–65)

In the year of Our Lord's incarnation 849, Alfred, king
of the Anglo-Saxons, was born at the royal village of
Wantage, in Berkshire, which county takes its name from
the wood of Berroc, where the box-tree grows most
abundantly.

Asser's *Life of Alfred*

THIS was the world into which Alfred was born, the youngest
son of the royal house of Cerdic which ruled Wessex. The
next half-century was likely to prove a testing time for the West
Saxon kings, but four lives lay between Alfred and the throne. His
elder brothers would no doubt bear the brunt. Like all early kings
the rulers of Wessex claimed a high ancestry, and at night, when the
torches were lit and the fire burnt up in the centre of one of the
wooden halls that were called "palaces", Alfred heard recited the
past glories of his family.

Alfred's father Ethelwulf traced his line back to King Ine
through five generations, and then beyond Ine, in theory at least,
to Cerdic, the fifth-century founder of Wessex—eight generations. And Cerdic, as every one knew, traced *his* descent from the
heathen god, Odin—five generations. The adoption of Christianity had extended the family tree backwards in time beyond
Odin so that it now began triumphantly with Adam. Such abori-
ginal ancestors were a commonplace for the Saxon kings. Divine
right was more than a political theory—it was a genealogical
fact.

Cealwin, at all events, ruler of Wessex from about 560 to 591
was a historical figure. He is the second in a list of seven kings
recorded by Bede as being rulers of Britain, with the slightly
mysterious title of *Bretwalda*, or "Britain-ruler". Certainly a
formal honour, it is not clear how far the real power of these
kings extended. Cealwin seems in fact to have been rather a small

THE ROYAL HOUSE OF WESSEX

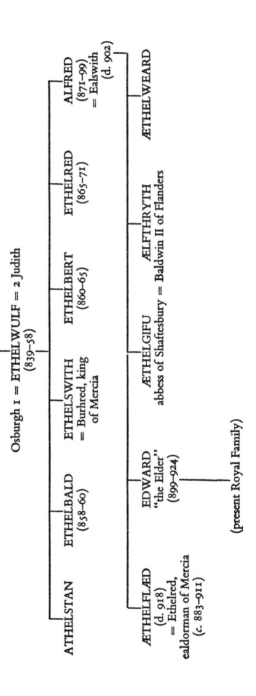

EGBERT
(802–39)

Osburgh 1 = ETHELWULF = 2 Judith
(839–58)

ATHELBALD
(858–60)

ETHELSWITH
= Burhred, king
of Mercia

ETHELBERT
(860–65)

ETHELRED
(865–71)

ALFRED
(871–99)
= Ealswith
(d. 902)

ATHELSTAN

EDWARD
"the Elder"
(899–924)

ÆTHELGIFU
abbess of Shaftesbury

ÆLFTHRYTH
= Baldwin II of Flanders

ÆTHELWEARD

ÆTHELFLÆD
(d. 918)
= Ethelred,
ealdorman of Mercia
(c. 883–911)

(present Royal Family)

fish. His real importance, and perhaps his contemporary reputation, rests on a single victory over the British at Dyrham in 577.

The village of Dyrham lies at the foot of the Cotswolds a few miles north of Bath and just to the west of the Bath–Cheltenham road. The victory opened the vale of the lower Severn to the Saxons, and split the lands of the Britons, cutting off those in Wales from their fellow countrymen in Somerset, Devon and Cornwall. It brought the forces of the invaders to the western shores of the island for the first time.

Cealwin's victory set the kingdom of Wessex on the road to power. Its rulers, it is true, soon lost control of the lower Severn to the Mercians, but in the south-west peninsula there was land for the taking. A miniature "colonial empire" could be acquired without the necessity for fighting fellow Saxons. By the middle of the seventh century they had conquered lowland Somerset and reached the western hill-country.

Towards the end of the seventh century Cædwalla, a younger member of the royal house, in a three years' whirlwind campaign overran the Isle of Wight, Sussex and Kent. He harried the island, slaughtering the local inhabitants—they were Jutes, another branch of the Saxon race—and replacing them by settlers from the Wessex mainland. Then with equal suddenness the young blood-stained man of violence made a pilgrimage to Rome. There, on Easter Day 689, he was baptized Peter. Ten days later he was dead. (The archbishop of Milan composed an epitaph in Latin verse for him.)

The pattern recurs. This combination of military ability and religious enthusiasm is one of the hallmarks of the kings of Wessex. Rome, in particular, drew them like a magnet.

Cædwalla's successor was Ine (688–726), the first great ruler of Wessex. The recently-conquered lands of Sussex and Kent were lost, but in the west Ine made great and permanent gains, the British kingdom of Dumnonia (Devon) was conquered and the frontiers of the kingdom pushed as far as the Tamar. The newly-conquered lands in Somerset to the west of the great forest of Selwood were civilized. Churches were built, and a bishopric created at Sherborne. The town of Taunton was established. Of equal importance was Ine's codification of the laws—a foundation on which Alfred later built.

Abruptly, in 726, King Ine abdicated, made the pilgrimage to Rome and, conforming to type, died there in retirement.

For almost a century after his death the kingdom of Wessex lapsed into obscurity. It fell under the overlordship of Mercia and even the names of its kings are now uncertain. Then, in the early ninth century, the interrupted line of development was taken up again.

The restorer of the fortunes of Wessex was Alfred's grandfather Egbert (802–839). While the Mercian king's protégé, Beorhtric, ruled in Wessex, Egbert—who was of the royal house and whose father had been a sub-king in Kent—was exiled as a dangerous man. For three years he lived at the court of the Emperor Charles the Great. On the death of Beorhtric, Egbert returned to England but for thirteen years after his accession to the throne he, like Brer Fox, seems to have preferred to "lay low and say nuffin". At all events, the records are silent save for one brief mention of a raid into Cornwall.

Then, late in his reign, Egbert suddenly burst into life and in four lightning campaigns, fought in the years 825 and 829, he made Wessex the strongest state in Britain.

The critical battle was the first, fought against his Mercian overlords at Ellendun, by the modern village of Nether Wroughton just south of Swindon. The area had long been a debatable ground between the two states. Egbert completely defeated the Mercians, "and," says the Chronicler, "there was a great slaughter made there." Immediately after the victory Egbert despatched his young son Ethelwulf against the Mercian puppet-states of Kent, Surrey, Sussex and Essex. Ethelwulf was brilliantly successful. He defeated the sub-king of Kent with no apparent effort, and the men of the other areas readily submitted, perhaps remembering their old links with Wessex.

There was still better news to come. The people of East Anglia who had been brought within the Mercian sphere of influence took heart at the news of this liberation of the lands beyond their southern frontier. They too "sought the peace and protection of King Egbert" and when Beornwulf, king of the Mercians, led an army against them, they killed him.

Thus in one year Egbert had destroyed the Mercian empire, added Kent, Surrey and Sussex (never again to be lost by Wessex) to his own lands, and become the overlord of Essex and East Anglia. After this *annus mirabilis* it is hardly surprising that there was a four years' pause for re-grouping.

Then, in 829, Egbert struck again. He swept through Mercia with his forces and forced the kingdom to accept his overlordship. He was now master of all England south of the Humber.

There remained only one independent Saxon kingdom: Northumbria. In the same year in which he overran Mercia, Egbert met the Northumbrian army at Dore, in Derbyshire, "and there," says the *Chronicle*, "they offered him submission and peace, and with that they separated." It was a remarkable situation; in four years Wessex had moved out of the shadow of Mercia, and had taken over her position as the most important state in England, one to which all the others owed nominal allegiance.

In 830, Egbert turned his attention to the Welsh "and he reduced them to humble submission".

Another pause followed and then in 838, in the last year of his life, Egbert led his victorious army into half-subdued West Wales. At Hingston Down on the high ground to the west of the River Tamar, he met and defeated a combined force of insurgent Cornish and pillaging Vikings. It was the final blow to Cornish independence.

The king's armies had won victories from the Trent to Land's End; Egbert struck coins with the proud inscription "King of the Mercians", and he became the first ruler to be hailed as *Bretwalda* in his lifetime. But the achievement, as always in those days, depended on the man himself. There is evidence that within a year or two of his death Mercia had recovered its independence.

Yet Egbert's victories had laid the permanent foundations of the later power of Wessex. In the east his acquisition of Kent and the adjoining provinces had made him protector of Canterbury, with all that that carried with it in terms of spiritual prestige. It had also brought his dynasty into a more intimate relationship with the continent. In the west he had completed the longdrawn-out conquest of the Britons of Devon and Cornwall. In short, he had created a kingdom that would, under Alfred, prove itself able to resist the Danes.

When Egbert died in 839 he was succeeded by his son Ethelwulf (839–858). What sort of a man was the new king, Alfred's father? In his youth he had proved himself an able leader and ruler. In later life the Viking raids pressed heavily upon his mind and, like so many of his house, he was drawn to Rome. He contracted a second marriage, strange and unsatisfactory. His thegns muttered and plotted against him and he was forced to put aside some of his royal power.

That lay in the future. When he became king men remembered how he had, together with the bishop of Sherborne and the ealdorman[1] of Hampshire, led the army which had recovered the lost provinces of Kent, Surrey, Sussex and Essex. When, after the victory, these areas had submitted to his father, Ethelwulf had ruled them as a kind of viceroy. Now that he was king he gave them in his turn to *his* eldest son, Athelstan, to administer.

Alfred's father appears to have been efficient, religious, and lacking in ambition. Fighting and ruling were for him the tiresome consequences of having been born to rule, a duty not a pleasure. Yet he dealt with the increasing pressure from the Viking sea-raiders with reasonable success.

The pirates' dragon-beaked ships had been appearing off the British islands for half a century, slipping up a creek here, beaching on the hard shingle there, always looting and burning. They were nothing new. What was novel and disturbing was the increasing frequency of the raids and the signs of large-scale organization behind them.

In 842 Vikings ravaged London and Rochester. Three years later Ethelwulf called out the levies of Somerset and Dorset to hold back an attack from the Bristol Channel on the Parrett estuary. In the winter of 850, the Viking longships lay up at the isle of Thanet. This was the first time they had wintered in England. The danger was growing.

For the moment the men of Wessex beat the Vikings back. Athelstan, in his capacity as ealdorman of Kent, defeated a Viking force near Sandwich, capturing nine ships and sending the others packing. While Athelstan was repelling this attack the king and his second son Ethelbald were marching to meet the main Danish army which had already stormed Canterbury and London and defeated the king of the Mercians.

[1] Ealdormen were appointed by the king, their sphere of jurisdiction was the shire.

In this crisis the blood of Egbert told. Ethelwulf vanquished the invaders "and," the *Anglo-Saxon Chronicle* records with enthusiasm, "made the greatest slaughter among the heathen host that we have ever heard tell of to this present day." It was indeed the most decisive Saxon victory between the days of Egbert and those of Alfred. The fleet that had stormed London numbered 350 ships and thirty men was not a great number for a Viking crew, so their army may well have numbered anything up to 10,000 fighting-men—a very large force for those days.

It would be pleasant to know exactly where Ethelwulf won his victory. The records give the name of the site as "Aclea" and imply that it was in Surrey. There *is* an Ockley there, but unfortunately the earliest form of the name seems to rule it out. The most likely candidate for the honour is Oakleigh, near Gravesend—but, as so often with the battles of the period, we cannot be certain.

A victory had been won, but nevertheless the Viking pressure continued to increase. Perhaps, Ethelwulf mused, God was displeased? In the minds of the men of those days, He still played a very active part in affairs of state and showed His displeasure in no uncertain manner. (When the tower of Winchester Cathedral fell down in 1101 no one was in the least surprised. Had not the ungodly corpse of William Rufus been deposited there only a few months before? That, it would seem, was the way in which God worked, and everyone recognized that this was so.)

Now the king's mind ran back to the first year of his reign, and to an unkept vow. In that year one of his clergy had seen a vision, had received a warning. The gist of it was that

> If Christians do not repent quickly of their crimes and wickednesses, and do not observe the Lord's Day with much more reverence, a great and irresistible disaster will quickly overtake them. For three days and nights a thick cloud will cover the land, and then immediately afterwards the pagans will come with a vast number of ships, and will destroy with fire and sword the land, and the people themselves with all their possessions. Nevertheless, if the people are prepared to repent and abandon their sins by fasting and almsgiving they may succeed in avoiding all these disasters.

At that time Ethelwulf had vowed that he would make a pilgrimage to Rome, but a dozen years had gone by and the promise was still unfulfilled. The house of Wessex had, as has been seen, something of a tradition of pilgrimages to Rome. He ought to go. . . . Yet this critical period was perhaps not the best time for the king himself to leave his kingdom.

These seem to have been the motives which prompted Ethelwulf to send his youngest son, Alfred, to Rome in 853—although, as Sir John Spelman cautiously commented in the seventeenth century, "What was Æthelwulf's direct purpose herein, we may diversely conjecture, but not determine."

Alfred was four years old at the time! Perhaps, as the youngest member of the royal family, he was regarded as expendable.

Ethelwulf had married Alfred's mother Osburh, about the year 835. Not very much is known about her. She came of Jutish stock from the recently reconquered territory of Kent. Her father was the king's seneschal, in charge of the royal household, but of high birth, being able to trace his descent from both Cerdic, the founder of the royal house of Wessex, and from the Jutish rulers of Kent.

Alfred's biographer Asser describes Queen Osburh as "a very devout woman, noble both by birth and by nature". Behind this perhaps conventional description she remains a shadowy figure. Later events indicate that she must have died in 854 or 855.

Five of her children survived infancy. The four sons Ethelbald, Ethelbert, Ethelred and Alfred each in turn ruled Wessex. The daughter, Ethelswith, was probably next in age to Ethelbald.

This is perhaps the place to say something about Saxon personal names, which look confusingly similar and slightly comic to a twentieth-century eye. The element *Ethel* (strictly *Æthel*) signified "noble", "of high birth". "Alfred", the exception, means—surprisingly—"elf-counsel". The elves in Saxon heathen times were the creative and sustaining spirits of nature, of the air, the earth, the countryside, and the prefix *Alf* was common in the royal families of Northumbria and East Anglia, though not in Wessex. Perhaps, since he was the youngest, his mother had been allowed to name Alfred, for the *Os* element in her own name referred to similar nature-spirits, the Anses, who were often coupled with the elves.

For Alfred the year 853 must have been full of uncomprehended but colourful happenings, for in the spring, before his visit to

Rome, his sister Ethelswith's wedding took place. After the
Easter celebrations she was married to Burhred, the new king of
Mercia, at the royal manor of Chippenham in Wessex. She cannot have been more than nine or ten at the time. Her future was
black. The little girl was later to see her new home conquered by
the Danes and to be deserted by her husband, who died a refugee
in far-off Italy.

After the wedding, in the summer, a large retinue left England
to escort Alfred on the hazardous journey to Rome. The distance
was immensely great and, added to the normal risks of travel in
those days, there were novel dangers. The Channel was full of
pirates, and the north European plain full of marauding bands of
Vikings. Last Christmas they had threatened the emperor and his
brother in Paris. This summer they were working up the Loire.
Nantes—Poitiers—Tours—one after another went up in flames.

Alfred and his convoy came through unharmed however.
Assuming that they took the normal route, they must have
crossed from Sandwich to somewhere near Le Touquet. (There
was a port on the River Canche known as Quentavic.) From
there the most likely route would have been by way of Paris,
Lyons and the western Alps to the comparative security of the
north Italian plain. Then south across the peaceful Apennines to
Rome.

The impact of Rome on a little boy must have been enormous.
The walls were fresh and shining, for the city had been sacked a
few years earlier by the Moors and the new fortifications had
only been completed the year before. On the 27th June in that
year Pope Leo IV, bare-foot and with ashes on his head, had led
the procession of dedication along the ramparts, and had prayed
that "this City which I, Thy servant Leo the Fourth, have dedicated . . . and which from my name is now called Leonine, may
ever remain unharmed and secure."

Within the Leonine walls there was so much to amaze a child
from Saxon England: the great ruined pillars of the Roman
Forum; the newly-decorated Romanesque Cathedral of St. Peter;
the great castle built over seven hundred years ago by the Roman
emperor Hadrian; the shrines and streets; and, towering over all,
the ruins of the Colosseum. "When the Colosseum falls, Rome
shall fall; and when Rome falls, the world falls," men said. It was

all so different from England where the palaces were wooden barns and the churches square stone boxes lit by narrow slits.

In the hot Italian sun pilgrims and traders from the whole world jostled along the streets. In England there were not even any streets.

Not everyone, of course, was impressed with *Romeburh*, as the northerners called it. A disillusioned Irishman wrote: "To go to Rome, much labour, little profit: the King whom thou seekest there, unless thou bring Him with thee, thou findest Him not. Much folly, much frenzy." But, for a child of four or five . . .

When the embassy left Rome, it carried back a letter from Pope Leo to Alfred's father:

> I have gladly received your son Alfred, whom you were anxious to send at this time to the precincts of the Holy Apostles, and as my spiritual son I had him girded with the honour and the outward trappings of nobility after the manner of the consuls at Rome, because he has given himself into my hands.

Describing the same events, the *Anglo-Saxon Chronicle* baldly and boldly states:

> . . . king Ethelwulf sent his son Alfred to Rome. Then was the lord Leo Pope in Rome, and he hallowed him to king and took him as bishop's son.

What really happened to Alfred? It is most unlikely that there was any sort of coronation, however much the writers of the *Chronicle* might later like to think so. Two ceremonies appear to have taken place, one spiritual, the other secular. At one the Pope acted as Alfred's sponsor at his confirmation—the boy became his "spiritual son", or "bishop's son". At the other, the Pope conferred on Alfred the secular dignity of "consul". This was an honorific title which the Pope gave relatively frequently at this time. Alfred was girded with a sword and, since the original ceremony was now heavily over-laid with Byzantine splendour, symbolically crowned and invested with a cloak of white and purple. These were the "outward array of nobility" referred to in Leo's letter.

To a worldly citizen of Rome it was a cheap honour designed

to impress ex-colonials, a diplomatic gesture to an outlying province. And the Saxon thegns, watching open-mouthed, were duly impressed as they were intended to be. Yet it was not perhaps entirely an empty ceremony. The psychological impact on a small, susceptible boy of the great cavernous building, the flaring candles and the spice-laden incense, the splendour and the heavy silk, must have been immense and—perhaps—lasting.

Yet if the journey to Rome had been designed to avert God's vengeance then it must have seemed to Ethelwulf that it had signally failed in its purpose. Alfred came back with the Pope's letter, but all through the winter and into the following year the Vikings stayed on the Isle of Sheppey, ready to launch fresh raids on England when the new campaigning season opened in the spring.

So now Ethelwulf decided that he must go himself to Rome. His wife, Alfred's mother Osburh, had just died and, in the light of what was to follow, one may guess that this also had something to do with his decision.

Perhaps, too, a wave of that religious enthusiasm which kept reappearing in the house of Wessex had swept over the king. For, before he left England, he granted the tenth part of his land by charter "to the praise of God and for his eternal health" to the service of religion. Nevertheless, it was a strange time to choose to be absent from his kingdom for over a year and in fact his action nearly brought disaster to Wessex.

It must have been in the year before her death that the only recorded episode in Queen Osburh's life took place. She was in the habit of reading Anglo-Saxon poems to her children. One day, says Asser,

> his mother showed Alfred and his brothers a book of Saxon poetry which she had in her hand, and said: 'I will give this book to whichever of you can learn it soonest.' Excited by these words, or rather by Divine inspiration, and attracted by the beautiful initial letter of the book, Alfred spoke before his brothers (his seniors in years but not in grace) and said: 'Will you really give that book to the one of us who can first understand and repeat it to you?' Smiling, his mother said: 'Yes, I will'. Then he immediately took the book out of her hand and went to his master to read it. Then Alfred brought it back to his mother and recited it.

In another place Asser says that Alfred remained "illiterate" until he was over eleven. At the time of the episode with his mother, Alfred was five or six. What happened then was that he learnt the poems by heart. Anyone who has read illustrated books to children knows how they associate the appearance of the page with the words on it, and can "read" each page as they turn to it.

Very soon after this Queen Osburh died, and Ethelwulf set off on his journey to Rome, taking Alfred with him. In Paris they were entertained by Charles the Great's grandson, Charles the Bald, king of the West Franks, who provided an escort for them as far as the frontier.

At Rome affairs were in a state of chaos. The old Pope Leo IV, Alfred's godfather, had died in July. Papal elections were always liable to turn into Roman riots and for three days there was fighting in the streets between the supporters of the new Pope, Benedict III, and those of the rival and defeated candidate, Anastasius. At one point Benedict was seized by the opposing faction. His vestments were torn off and he was beaten and imprisoned. Eventually, however, the followers of Anastasius were routed, and Benedict was duly consecrated in the autumn. The Saxon pilgrims arrived in the city while all this was going on.

Ethelwulf and Alfred remained in Rome for over a year. The *Book of the Popes* gives a list of the gifts that the king had brought to Rome: silver to be thrown to the common people; gold for the clergy and nobles; for the Pope a crown of pure gold, a sword ornamented with gold, together with a dalmatic and alb of gold and silver thread and white silk; for the Roman churches, candelabra, and four silver-gilt hanging lamps for use as sanctuary lights.

Later traditions maintain that Ethelwulf also revived the payment originally made to Rome by King Offa and later known as "Peter's Pence" and that he helped to restore the Saxon School in Rome (now the Church and Hospital of San Spirito). The quarter on the Vatican Hill that stretched from the circus of Nero to the River Tiber was filled with the settlements not only of English, but of other "Saxons"—Germans, Frisians, Franks and so on. The area had been destroyed by fire a few years before and was gradually being rebuilt. As a consequence of his action Ethelwulf makes an appearance in Raphael's fresco of the fire, standing next to

Godfrey of Bouillon, and identified by the inscription "Astulphus, king of England came here and paid tribute".

In the following spring Ethelwulf and Alfred began the homeward journey, and now, instead of hurrying back to an England threatened by continual Viking raids, Ethelwulf broke his journey again at the court of Charles the Bald and remained there—the weeks extending into months. Then at last all was made clear. In July it was announced that the king, now a man in his fifties, was to marry Charles the Bald's daughter, Judith, who was about twelve years old.

Was this passion or policy? Charles and Ethelwulf might both benefit from an alliance sealed by a dynastic marriage. On the whole the Frankish king needed allies even more than did the king of Wessex. The Vikings and Saracens were raiding as usual (the former were back on the Seine in August), and Brittany and Aquitaine were both in revolt against Charles' overlordship. Even a Saxon kinglet would be a useful ally, especially if his lands bordered on the Channel. So much for policy.

On the other hand, there is evidence to suggest that Judith's blood held a strong attraction for men. Her grandmother (also called Judith) had been a famous beauty in her day and a thorn in the side of her husband, the Emperor Louis. The second Judith also was destined to have a chequered matrimonial life.

The wedding of the old Saxon king and the adolescent Frankish princess took place on 1st October at Verberie-sur-Oise, near Compiègne. The ceremony was performed by the great Hincmar, scholar and archbishop of Rheims.

What followed was, to the eyes of an age scrupulous in tradition, a worse scandal. Judith was anointed and crowned by Hincmar as queen consort equal in dignity to the king—a title that was clean contrary to West Saxon custom. In general the Saxons kept their women-folk in the background. This habit had received, in the case of the West Saxons, powerful support from the behaviour of Queen Eadburh, less than a century ago. She had reigned as an equal, and her husband had died of poison—prepared, *she* said, for her enemies. Nevertheless she had found it wise to flee the country and, after failing as an abbess (she was deprived of her position for misbehaviour) died a beggar-woman. A bad omen.

What, one wonders, did Alfred feel as he watched the coronation of his girl stepmother? The original wording of the service has survived. As Judith was crowned queen-consort, Hincmar prayed:

> The Lord crown thee with glory and honour and place upon thy head the precious stones of the Spirit; that the glitter of gold and sparkle of jewels here may be a token of the glory which may ever shine forth in thee and in thy doings; Which things may He Himself vouchsafe to grant, to Whom is honour and glory for ever and ever, Amen.
> Bless, O Lord, this Thy servant: Thou Who from all time dost rule the realms of Kings, Amen.

The solemn, half-understood words echoed in the boy's mind.

Ethelwulf, together with his new queen and Alfred, now came home to England. It was not a moment too soon, for power was slipping from the king's grasp. His eldest son Athelstan was dead, and his second son Ethelbald was laying plans to prevent his father's return. With the help of Ealhstan, bishop of Sherborne, and Eanwulf, the ealdorman of Somerset, he tried, says Asser, "to commit the great crime of stopping the king from coming into his own kingdom".

The reasons are obvious: Ethelwulf's continued absence from the kingdom when it was a king's duty to be concerned in the day-to-day management of affairs (for even the most stable kingdoms soon lapsed into disorder if the king was away for long); the alienation of a tenth of the crown lands; the news of the young queen treated as an equal; the ambition of the king's son, a passionate, impetuous man—these are the motives which lie behind the general comment of Asser:

> ... many think it was due solely to the pride of the king (Ethelwulf's son) because that king was headstrong and did many other perverse acts beside this.

It was a critical moment for the kingdom. If civil war broke out, Wessex might slip into Northumbrian anarchy, at the very moment when the Viking menace was increasing. The danger was that the conspirators would hold western Wessex, while the king triumphed in the east, and that in consequence the kingdom would split in two. Not all the skill of Alfred could then have saved either portion from the Danes. But the conspirators failed to carry the nobles with them and Ethelwulf—either from fear or out of policy—was prepared to compromise. Asser continues:

> To prevent the irreparable evil of the whole nation carrying on civil war, by the extraordinary forbearance of the father and with the consent of all the nobles, the kingdom was divided between father and son. The eastern districts were given to the father, and the western to the son.

So Ethelbald lorded it in the west, in Wessex proper, and the old king reigned in the east, in Sussex, Surrey, Kent and Essex. And to the scandal of all right-thinking Saxons Judith sat on the throne at his side.

Two years later, in 858, Ethelwulf died in peace and was buried in the old church at Winchester. He was not destined to remain in peace however. In the twelfth century Bishop Henry of Blois collected the king's bones, together with those of other Saxon and Danish rulers, and put them in mortuary chests. In the sixteenth century these chests were placed on the north and south Choir Screens by Bishop Fox. Then, in the next century, came the Civil War. In December 1642 a troop of Roundhead horse rode into Winchester Cathedral and up the longest nave in England to the choir. Dismounting, they set to work. They broke up the altar and tore down the organ. They defaced the statues. Then they toppled down the mortuary chests "and scattered the bones all over the pavement". At the Restoration the chests were piously restored to their position in the Choir—they are there today—but the bones of Saxon Ethelwulf are now inextricably mingled with those of, among others, the Danish king Canute.

In his will Ethelwulf divided the kingdom between Ethelbald and his third son, Ethelbert. One poor man was to be fed and clothed from every ten hides of the crown lands that were under cultivation. A sum of three hundred mancuses (each mancus was valued at thirty pence—the price of an ox) were to be sent to Rome each year, two-thirds to supply oil for the lamps in the churches of St. Peter and St. Paul at Easter, and one-third for the Pope's personal use.

The provisions of the will throw some light on the old king's

state of mind in these last years, but otherwise are of little significance, for there is no evidence that they were observed by his
successor.

Immediately upon his accession Ethelbald married his stepmother, the beautiful Judith, now a young woman of about sixteen, "infamously sharing with him in his Bed, as well as in his
Kingdom," Spelman writes indignantly. An act "contrary to the
law of God and the dignity of a Christian, contrary even to all
pagan custom," exclaims the scandalized Asser, who continues
that the king "drew down upon himself infamy from all who
heard about it." Fortunately, perhaps, for Wessex Ethelbald died
prematurely two years later, and was buried at Sherborne. His
bones, together with those of his younger brother and successor
Ethelbert, probably lie below the floor-level in the North Aisle
of Sherborne Abbey, where they can now be seen, rather oddly,
by push-button lighting.

On his elder brother's death Ethelbert (860–865) became king
of all Wessex, uniting the two parts once more. The already
twice-widowed Judith was packed off back to France. Her father
lodged her in the castle of Senlis a few miles from the church
where she had been crowned queen-consort only five years
before. There she was visited by Baldwin the "Iron-Arm", later
count of Flanders and, helped by her brother, Judith eloped with
Baldwin and fled to Rome. Her furious father persuaded the
French bishops to excommunicate her lover, but the Pope,
Nicholas I, was more sympathetic. In the end the king gave way—
but he refused to attend the wedding! Thirty years later one of
Alfred's daughters, Aelfthryth, married the son of Judith and
Baldwin.

In the first year of Ethelbert's reign Vikings crossed from the
neighbourhood of the Somme and sailed up the River Itchen to
Winchester. They plundered the city, but were put to flight by
the ealdormen of Hampshire and Berkshire, Osric and Ethelwulf.
(The latter, a powerful fighter, was later to help Alfred.) For the
remainder of Ethelbert's short life there was comparative peace—
but it was a deceptive peace, the moment of quiet before the
storm broke for good upon England, and upon Alfred.

For in 865 Ethelbert died and was buried at Sherborne. The
royal family of Wessex was rapidly shrinking in numbers and

Alfred moved into the foreground of the picture. Once the youngest of five brothers, he was now next in importance to the new king, his brother Ethelred (865–71). Ethelred had two sons of his own, but they were infants, while Alfred, now sixteen, was by the standards of those days a grown man. His brother recognized the logic of the situation and Alfred was officially declared to be *secundarius*, second-in-command, and perhaps with some implication in the title of a right to succeed to the throne. If the new king died before his sons grew up a man would have to rule in Wessex. And that man could only be Alfred.

History, so often without a sense of plot, seemed on this occasion to have synchronized the arrival of the man and the hour. For the *Anglo-Saxon Chronicle* entry in 865 runs as follows:

> Here Ethelred, Ethelbert's brother, succeeded to the kingdom of the West-Saxons; *and the same year the Great Army came to the land of the English* and took up their winter-quarters in East Anglia and there they were supplied with horses; and the men of East Anglia made peace with them.

What was this Great Army? It was the largest Viking force that had yet reached England and it had come not to ravage, but to take the country. Moreover, to make matters worse, the kingdom of East Anglia was apparently prepared to accept—or at any rate not to resist—the heathen. In view of the Vikings' reputation one can understand the East Anglians' attitude. This critical situation explains Alfred's appointment as *secundarius*. It is time to consider more closely what manner of men the Vikings were, for Alfred was to struggle against the Great Army—and other "Great Armies"—for the rest of his life.

Ravens from the East

. . . the promiscuous Vent of all *Germany*, and for the most
part the Refuse Scumm of all the Maritime Parts thereof,
. . . who rejecting Labour and civil Habitation gave themselves to no other Course of Life, nor sought they other
Sustenation, than only Theft, Robbery and Violence . . .
Sir John Spelman, 1643

SOME time in the summer of 787 the king's reeve at Dorchester
heard that three strange ships had come in to shelter at Portland
Bill and were beached there. He saddled his horse and rode over to
see, as was his duty, what sort of people had landed there and to
take them to the king's town. The strangers cut him down where
he stood. Perhaps they left the mark of the raven upon him, sepa-
rating his ribs from his breast bone and spreading them out so that
they formed a grim heraldic caricature, dripping blood, of a bird's
wings. It was a common habit of theirs.

That was the first English experience of the Vikings. The event
is described in the bare prose of the *Anglo-Saxon Chronicle* as
follows:

> In the days of king Beorhtric first came three ships of the Northmen
> from Horthaland. Then the royal reeve rode thither and tried to
> compel them to go to the king's town, for he did not know what
> they were; and they slew him. These were the first ships of the Danes
> to come to England.

The event made such an impact on the men of Wessex that, a
hundred and fifty years later, this isolated event, a single morning's
activity, was still being described in circumstantial detail:

> While good king Beorhtric reigned in Wessex, and the people
> were scattered innocently through the plains, enjoying themselves
> in tranquillity and yoking their oxen to the plough, a small fleet of
> three Danish long-ships suddenly arrived. When the king's reeve who

was then in Dorchester heard it, he leaped on his horse and galloped with a few men to the port, thinking that they were merchants not enemies. He addressed them in a commanding tone and ordered them to go to Dorchester. But he was killed on the spot and all those that were with him. The name of the reeve was Beaduherd.

The event deserved to be remembered, for it marked a new epoch in the history of England. For almost three hundred years our history was to be interwoven with that of the Scandinavians. And not English history only. The Viking invasions which dominate the reign of Alfred were only part of a much larger movement that affected and afflicted the whole of north-western Europe.

The name "Vikings" was a general term for raiding forces of Danes, Norsemen and Swedes. The original meaning is no longer known for certain, but derives either from the word for a camp (temporary camps being a common feature of Viking raids) or more probably from the Norse word *vik*, a creek or inlet. These "creek-hunters" were the last pagans in western Europe.

Their raids began in the eighth century and dominated the ninth to such an extent that it has been called "the Viking century". They represent the final great movement westwards of Nordic man before the settlement of the east coast of America in the seventeenth century.

To their victims they were just "Vikings" or "Norsemen", but there were three distinct routes of expansion and these corresponded approximately to modern national divisions. The ancestors of the Swedes moved east and south up the rivers which lead from the Baltic into the heart of Russia. They gave that country its name, derived from the Finnish word for Swedes, *Ruotsi*, and ruled there till the thirteenth century. From Russia some pushed on to Byzantium, which they knew as *Micklegarth*, "the great city". There they entered the emperor's service and formed the famous, feared, Varangian Guard.

Westward expansion followed two routes. The Norwegians sailed in general to the north of the British Isles. They went by way of the Faroes to Iceland—in the tenth century there were 20,000 settled there. From Iceland they colonized Greenland, and from Greenland they made isolated voyages to North America. It was an astounding achievement.

Other Norwegians chose to attack, and ultimately settle in, the northern and western coasts of the British Isles. Their impact was considerable. In the Shetlands Norwegian survived as a living language until the end of the eighteenth century, and the islanders still celebrate the Norse winter festival, Up-helly-aa. They ruled the Orkneys until 1468 and the most northern county in Scotland is still called Sutherland, "the southern land", because it lay to the south of these Viking conquests. The Norwegians sailed on round the north of Scotland to Ireland, and carved out a kingdom for themselves, ruling there from 853 to 1014. The wife of the first ruler was enthroned as a pagan prophetess before the high altar of Clonmacnois, the most holy place in Ireland.

It was the third route, the southern one leading to Saxon England, that was taken by the Danes. They sailed up the rivers of western Europe from Flanders to Spain. Their ships appeared, far from the open sea, on the Seine, the Loire, the Garonne, the Guadalquivir and they sacked the cities and monasteries that lined the banks. Paris was besieged four times. Their dragon-beaked ships were moored beneath the walls of Nantes and Bordeaux. The marauders sacked the monastery of Luxeuil, lying in the heart of France 270 miles from the nearest salt water. They passed the pillars of Hercules and terrorized the western Mediterranean— Charles the Great is said to have wept when he saw their long ships there—burning and looting as far as Pisa in western Italy.

But, above all, the Danes crashed like ocean waves against the shores of Britain from Northumbria down the east coast and through the Channel to southern Ireland. For Saxon England lay at the centre of this great tornado of Scandinavian energy, and on her ability to resist its force would turn the fate of northwest Europe. In that resistance lies one part of the significance of Alfred's reign, one justification for his title of "the Great".

What caused this explosion of Viking activity, as unexpected as it was successful? Why did these men suddenly start to seek their fortunes overseas? This is, unfortunately, one of the great unanswered questions of history. There is no clear, generally accepted explanation. Too many men on too few acres in a bare and unproductive land was certainly a cause—probably the major one. Then, too, the establishment of law and order in ninth-century Denmark by King Horic clearly made life unendurable there for many younger sons and wilder spirits. The destruction by the Emperor Charles the Great of two buffer-states to the south-east of Denmark, Saxony and Frisia, removed a barrier to Scandinavian expansion in the direction of the English Channel. In these facts lie the springs of the Norsemen's achievement.

The Viking character was curiously ambivalent. Because they stormed England one aspect of their nature has been emphasized at the expense of the other. They have had a bad press. Sir John Spelman sees them

> . . . practising the using of shipping for the love of Piracie, and like flights of Wasps and Hornets coasting all about, whatsoever fertile place by any was discovered the whole swarm soon seised upon it, and made a prey of the Plenty, sucking out the sweet of others Labours, and devouring whatsoever others industry had with their sweat prepared.

But there was another side to the Norsemen. They made almost a hobby of law-suits—the very word *law* is, amazingly, Old Norse. At home they were hunters and fishers, fur traders and farmers, and their merchants created a large port at Hedeby in south Denmark. They were artists in wood and metal work, fine craftsmen with a distinctive "abstract" style of their own. Above all, they were brilliant shipwrights.

Against this must be set the fact that they were savage and heathen. They had no written literature. For inscriptions they used a cumbersome alphabet, the Runic, which had no connection with the Latin characters of Romanized Europe. Their religion included the practice of human sacrifice.

The raiders had chosen a comfortless trade. Often they became men without a home, men who, as they said, "never slept beneath the sooty roof-beams, and never drank in the inglenook". Their hard religion taught that the world would end soon in an apocalyptic climax of fire and blood and battle and that they lived in "an age of axes, an age of sword, an age of wolves".

With such a creed, it is not surprising that in battle they went mad. Their leaders included *wolf-coats*, champions with animal strength, dressed in skins, and *berserks* (bareshirts, who fought without armour). The Ynglinga saga says of the berserks that they believed they were under the direct protection of their high god

Odin and therefore "they went without armour, and were mad as dogs or wolves, and bit their shields and were as strong as bears or bulls".

Strange and terrifying, they appeared like some new plague everywhere in the civilized west. Into the Litanies of their victims there was written in the ninth century a new petition: "From the fury of the Northmen, O Lord, deliver us."

The success of the Vikings depended on three factors. One was the unprepared state of the countries they attacked, and perhaps the least well able to defend itself was Saxon England—until the coming of Alfred. Another factor was the Viking character, tough and fearless, a curious compound of the reckless with the cautious and adaptable. It comes out especially clearly in the *Havamal*, a collection of proverbial sayings:

> Seek not to know thy fate, so shalt thou live most free from grief; but do not go out without your spear.

> The fool thinks he will live for ever if he avoids fighting: the spear may spare him, but age will not.

> The early man takes another's wealth—or his life.

> If you have an uncertain friend, address him with fair words but a crafty heart, and repay treachery with lies.

> Praise no day till evening, no wife until she is buried, no sword until tested, no maid until given in marriage, no ice until crossed, no ale until it has been drunk.

and finally:

> Cattle die, kinsfolk die, even to ourselves will death come. One thing I know will never die, the reputation we all leave behind on our death.[1]

The third factor on which the success of their raids rested was the Viking long-ship, a machine at once beautiful and perfectly adapted to its owners' needs—as elegant and efficient as an air-liner.

A great deal is known about these ships—more, probably, than

[1] B. S. Philpotts; *Edda and Saga*.

about any earlier European vessel. They are carved on Viking graves and stitched into the Bayeux tapestry. Beyond this some of the actual boats themselves have survived. They were buried under large mounds of earth to serve as the graves of chieftains and six or seven have been excavated. The best-known example was found at Gokstad, in Norway, in 1880.

The Gokstad ship was rather longer than a cricket pitch (76 ft. 6 ins. from stem to stern), with a beam of 17 ft. 6 ins. and —most important for the Viking raiders—although her depth was almost 7 ft. she drew only 2 ft. 9 ins. of water. The sides were clinker-built with sixteen overlapping oak planks caulked with animal hair. These planks were nailed one to another, but fastened to the ribs and keel by ties—a method of construction which gave the vessel great elasticity.

The ship was powered by sixteen oars on each side, varying in length from seventeen to nineteen feet (the shortest naturally being placed amidships). The rowlocks were holes cut in the ship's side and fitted with shutters that fell into place when the oars were shipped. There was a large bat-shaped steering board fixed high on the right-hand side aft—hence the modern term "starboard" for that side of a ship. Amidships was a strong mast up to forty feet high that could be taken down if required and which carried a large square sail.

There was no question of camouflage. Merchant ships might be grey and squat and might slink along the coast, anxious to escape detection, but the Viking warship blazed with colour from stem to stern. The sail was painted in broad stripes, the sides were coloured too, round bright shields hung along the gunwale, a flag streamed from the masthead, and at either end fierce, carved dragon-heads rose high into the air.

Such a long-ship was fast, seaworthy, and could be easily beached, or rowed up a river into the heart of the enemy's territory. She could stand up to the ocean rollers. In 1892 a copy of the Gokstad ship was constructed and a crew of Norwegians sailed her across the Atlantic. They took four weeks to make the crossing!

Normally the crew of such a ship would number about forty but there was room at a pinch for as many as eighty men. Their conditions of service have survived. The crews were drawn from men between the ages of 16 and 60 and they had to be able to fight as well as to sail the ship. They were not allowed to bring any women with them; they had to obey the captain in all things, reporting all news to him and accepting his judgements implicitly, especially in the controversial matter of the division of spoil.

The captain's quarters lay aft, where he could keep an eye on the steersman. Those next in rank occupied the bow, and it was there that the weapons and armour were stacked. A certain amount of equipment and plunder could also be stowed under the loose planking which formed the deck, but apart from that the crew had to make do with the narrow space between one rowing-bench and the next. Each man kept his personal gear in a wooden locker under the bench, and at night he curled up between the benches in his skin sleeping-bag. In harbour, or when becalmed, the sail could be taken down and slung fore and aft to make a sort of ridge-pole tent running the length of the ship.

These were the sort of ships that so unexpectedly sailed in out of the blue to Portland, and these were the men who cut down the king's reeve from Dorchester. The ships were probably off course, as a matter of fact, for the men were Norwegians not Danes, and the alarming incident remained, as far as southern England was concerned, an isolated experience not repeated for many years.

At much the same time there were far more serious raids on the coast of Northumbria. In the summer of 793 "heathen men" sacked St. Cuthbert's church at Lindisfarne. It had been the mother-church of Christianity in the north and when the Englishman Alcuin of York, who was then living on the continent at the court of Charles the Great, heard the news, he was appalled. "For almost 350 years," he wrote, "we and our fathers lived in that fair land, and never before have such terrors appeared in Britain as these . . . nor was it thought that such an inroad from the sea could be made." It was recalled that earlier in the year fiery dragons had been seen flying in the air!

> Men's cheeks faded
> On shores invaded
> When shorewards waded
>   The lords of fight;

When monks affrighted
To windward sighted
The birds full-flighted
Of swift sea-kings;

When churl and craven,
Saw hard on haven
The wide-winged raven
At main-mast height.

Next year the Norsemen came again and sacked the Northumbrian monastery of Jarrow. Monasteries were easy to take, and provided good pickings. On this occasion, however, all did not go smoothly. The Viking ships were caught in a storm. Many were sunk and their crews drowned; for the rest, as the *Anglo-Saxon Chronicle* laconically records, "some came to the shore alive and were straightway slain at the river's mouth."

And now for a time the danger seemed to have passed England by. The raiders were sailing far to the north, settling in Scotland and Ireland, sacking the monastery of Iona off Mull, but leaving the Saxon shores at peace.

Thirty years went by. In England a generation was born and grew to maturity in a land delusively secure and calm.

Then in 835 the raids began again and this time there was no respite. For two generations the Saxons fought to save their land from the men who were carving out kingdoms for themselves throughout Europe—in Russia, Normandy, Sicily, Ireland.

At first it was hit-and-run raiding. There is no continuous thread, but isolated events stand out in the *Chronicle*, great victories, disastrous defeats. In 842, the Danes sacked London. It was not the capital of a kingdom—it belonged to Mercia—but it was probably already the richest port and largest town in the island. "There was," records the *Chronicle*, "great slaughter at London." Meanwhile the exposed east coast of England was being raided yearly. Soon there was not a Saxon church left standing, it was said, within a day's ride of the sea.

This was bad, but there was worse to follow. About the middle of the century the Saxons observed two alarming developments in the pattern of the Viking attacks. The raids were no longer those of a few individuals looking for adventure and quick profits.

The fleets became too large and their operations too methodical for these to be the exploits of outlaws or pirates. There were signs that they had some sort of official or semi-official support.

The other development was even more ominous. So far the enemy had appeared only in the summer. The long-ships would sail in on the spring east winds, spend a profitable summer plundering, and then go home to Scandinavia on the prevailing west winds in the autumn. That had always been the pattern. Then in the year 850 autumn came and went, but the ships did not leave. A fleet spent all winter at Thanet, off the coast of Kent.

The Vikings had come to stay.

In the following spring a huge army—it came in 350 ships and so could possibly have numbered 10,000 men—sacked London and Canterbury, defeated the king of the Mercians and then moved into Surrey. For the first time a Viking army was loose in Wessex.

When the news was brought to Alfred's father Ethelwulf, he called out the men of Wessex and marched west with his son Ethelbald (the same son who later married his father's widow Judith). Ethelwulf was not Egbert's son for nothing. He destroyed the invading army of Danes at the already-mentioned battle of Aclea.

The *Chronicle* records the events of 850–1 as follows:

> . . . heathen men settled over winter in Thanet. And the same year came three hundred and fifty ships to the mouth of the Thames and stormed Canterbury and London and put to flight Behrtwulf king of the Mercians with his army and then fared south over the Thames and there Ethelwulf and his son Ethelbald with the army of the West Saxons fought against them at Aclea and there made the greatest slaughter among the heathen army that we ever heard tell up to this present day, and there gained the victory.

The battle of Aclea was a triumph for Ethelwulf and a portent for the future, but at the time it seemed an empty success. To try to hold back the Danes was like trying to check the sea—held in one place, they came in somewhere else.

For fifteen years the raiding grew in intensity and the pirates often wintered in the land. Then, in 865, there was a further turn of the screw. The Danes came, not to raid or to winter, but to conquer. For the next thirteen years the "Great Army" that landed in 865 marched and counter-marched and fought and conquered across the length and breadth of Saxon England.

The leaders of this army in the initial stages of its existence were two brothers, Halfdan and Ivar the Boneless, real men whose existence is recorded in a *mélange* of hard, dated facts and brightly coloured legend.

Their father, Ragnary Lothbrok ("Leather Breeches"—wearing a sort of cowboy's chaps cut off at the knee) had been the most famous Viking raider in the middle years of the century. It was he who had sailed up the Seine to Paris in 845, a distance of almost two hundred miles, while the armies of the Frankish king Charles the Bold followed impotently along the river banks. The inhabitants of the city watched in horror as he sacrificed one hundred and eleven prisoners before the walls of Paris. Then, on Easter Day, he stormed and sacked the palace. He took the ironwork from the city gate as a trophy, and his men hacked down beams from the church of St. Germain-des-Prés, and used them to repair their ships. And Charles, in theory one of the two most powerful rulers in Christendom, gave the heathen Ragnar seven thousand pounds of silver to go away. "Who would have believed," wrote the monk Paschasius, "which among us would have imagined, that that could happen which we have seen with our own eyes and wept over, the enemy entering our city of Paris and burning the churches of Christ on its river the Seine?"

In the fifties Ragnar's sons, a family of elusive buccaneers, took to raiding on their own account. They carried out a trial expedition to the Thames estuary; they followed in their father's footsteps up the Seine; they spoiled the monastery of St. Denis and forced its abbot, a grandson of the Emperor Charles the Great, to buy them off.

Now these formidable men had turned their attentions to England. The law of diminishing returns was operating. They were getting less loot from an already-plundered northern Europe, and facing growing resistance. Soon the continent might be too hot to hold them. England, however, was a relatively unworked field. And what chance of success could the little Saxon kingdoms have when the great Frankish state itself had failed to hold them off?

A hard, business-like assessment of possible gain seems thus to have been the real motive for the Great Army's arrival. A later story provided a more romantic explanation. Ragnar Leather-Breeches, it was said, was wrecked with only two ships on the coast of Northumbria. He and his men waded ashore and fought their way through the hostile countryside, living on what they could take.

When the news was brought to Ælle, king of Northumbria, he raised an army and marched from York against the little band. There was a hard fight, but the odds were too great and in the end the Danes were cut down. Ragnar—the old fox Ragnar—was taken alive. He was thrown at Ælle's command into a pit of adders. There he sat, and the snakes would not touch him. "Take off his coat", commanded Ælle. It was his wife's gift, a magic garment. Now the snakes wreathed him from head to foot, and as they did so Ragnar sang his death song:

> I have fought fifty battles and won, I never thought I would die in a snake-pit. . . . How the young pigs would grunt if they knew of the old boar's plight.

The saga goes on to tell how the "young pigs" received the news. The eldest, Bjorn, was holding his spear; he gripped the shaft so strongly that his fingers sank into it and left their print in the wood. Halfdan was playing chess—the Norsemen were surprisingly fond of this gentle game—and had picked up a pawn when the news came. His muscles contracted so that blood burst out round his nails. Sigurd "Snake-eye" was cutting his nails with a knife and went on unconsciously trimming them until he reached the bone!

There is obviously plenty of dramatic invention here, but myths have an odd way of being founded on historical fact. (One remembers Schliemann, that nineteenth-century German grocer, who took the *Iliad* at its face value, went and dug where the events it described were supposed to have occurred, and found the site of Troy.) Less than a hundred and fifty years after Ragnar's death, there existed a firm tradition that his sons had led the Great Army to England to seek revenge. It is not unreasonable to suppose that revenge and gain were twin motives in the minds of Halfdan and Ivar the Boneless. (Ivar, incidentally, got his peculiar nickname as follows: when Ragnar married Ivar's mother she begged him to wait three days before consummating the marriage, since a spell was on her. Ragnar refused, and their first child was in consequence born with gristle instead of bones.)

The year 865, when the Great Army landed, is a decisive date, marking the beginning of the Danish Conquest as clearly as the battle of Hastings marks the Norman conquest. It was also the decisive year in Alfred's life when his brother Ethelred declared Alfred, now sixteen, to be *secundarius*.

The first step had been taken on the road that led eventually to the title of "the Great".

Second in Command (865-71)

> And now, to use nautical language, I will no longer
> commit my vessel to the force of the waves and of its sails,
> nor, keeping away from land, steer roundabout through
> innumerable calamities of war and lists of years; but I will
> return instead to that which prompted me first to this task,
> that is to say I will now relate as much as I have learned
> about the boyhood of my revered master, Alfred, king of
> the Anglo-Saxons, as briefly and as fully as I possibly can.
>
> Asser's *Life of Alfred*

THIS would seem to be the place to describe in detail Alfred's
early life and upbringing. Unfortunately, in spite of Asser's
promise, the Bishop proceeds to tell us nothing apart from the
story of the poetry book given to Alfred by his mother, and the
fact that he subsequently learned "the daily Course", that is the
religious celebration of the hours, and afterwards certain psalms
and many prayers. But "with shame be it spoken, by the un-
worthy neglect of his parents and nurses, he remained illiterate
even till he was twelve years old or more".

Other than these remarks of Asser's, we really know nothing
of Alfred's life before the age of sixteen, except for the public
events already described: his birth at Wantage in 849; his first
journey to Rome in 853, when he was "crowned" by Pope Leo;
his second journey to Rome with his father, 855–6; and finally
his nomination as *secundarius* in 866.

It is possible, though, to reconstruct the kind of life that a young
Saxon prince such as Alfred led. Although the king was in one
sense, by virtue of his kingship, set apart from his followers and
thanes, in another sense he was only the first among equals. The
royal court was only a nobleman's household writ a little larger.
And so, except for a slightly greater standard of comfort, a tendency for daily life to be on a slightly larger scale, Alfred's early
years would be like those of any young nobleman of the time.

The king's estates were scattered throughout Wessex and the royal family travelled about their lands, living for a while at one manor, and then moving on to the next. They would journey, a draggle-tailed convoy of heavy carts chunking slowly along roads that were no better than modern farm-tracks, from Wantage to Winchester, the chief town in Wessex, dominated by the Old Minster and, when Alfred was a boy, dominated also by its bishop, St. Swithun. Dominated, though, is perhaps the wrong word for though the bishop was a great administrator it was reported he was so humble that he refused to ride on horseback but went everywhere on foot. Nevertheless, he was an important member of the Witan, the king's council, and is said to have had a hand in Ethelwulf's journey to Rome and in patching up the later peace with the king's rebellious son. He died in 861, when Alfred was twelve, and left orders that he was to be buried outside the cathedral "beneath the feet of passers-by and the rain dripping from the eaves". (In the next century the Bishop's body was moved inside—but the move was delayed by heavy rains for forty days!)

From Winchester the whole household would up traps and move on to Dorchester, where they seem often to have spent Christmas. North of Dorchester was Sherborne, a see that had been founded by King Ine for the newly-conquered lands of Somerset and the west. Easter was frequently spent at Wilton in Wiltshire, and from there the caravanserai could easily reach the royal manor of Chippenham close to the frontier with Mercia.

This peripatetic life served a double purpose. It enabled the king to keep an eye on his kingdom and to hear complaints in person. It was also the most convenient way of feeding the royal entourage.

The records speak of royal "palaces", but they were only large halls, usually timber-built. No Saxon palaces survive, indeed very few Saxon buildings of any sort are still standing. For one thing, the Saxons used mainly wood—to such an extent that they saw architecture as carpentry and even when they built in stone, they tended to handle the stone as if it were timber. Their wooden buildings have fallen down, their stone buildings have been replaced by later ones. What remains is mainly ecclesiastical, a handful of Saxon churches, a rather larger number of crypts, and for the rest an occasional patch of not very impressive masonry embedded in a later building. Of secular architecture there is nothing.

Or rather, there is nothing above ground. Recently, however, archaeologists have added considerably to our knowledge of Saxon domestic architecture. A seventh-century royal hall has been excavated at Yeavering in Northumberland, and the foundations of a Saxon hall—or rather a series of halls—have been discovered at Cheddar in Somerset. There was a royal manor there, and the earliest hall was in existence between 850 and 930. There is thus a reasonable presumption that it was in use in the time of Alfred.

The excavator, Mr. Philip Rahtz, found two walls of double post-holes (the outer holes vertical, the inner sloping), running in a north–south direction. The hall which these holes indicate was slightly boat-shaped, about 80 ft. long and 18 ft. wide at the widest point, narrowing to 16 ft. at the ends. There were two entrances opposite one another in the middle of the two long walls, and a possible smaller entrance at the end of one of the long walls. The sloping post-holes suggest the existence of a "first-floor" above ground-level. This appears to have been a not unusual feature of a great Saxon hall. The *Chronicle* records that in 978 "all the chief Witan fell at Calne from an upper chamber, except for archbishop Dunstan who was standing on a beam". It is not impossible that when Alfred later made the treaty of Wedmore with the Danes it was concluded in the hall at Cheddar.

One may imagine Alfred growing-up in these large, timber-built, barn-like structures, for apart from specialized activities such as cooking the hall formed what modern architects would call a "living-space" in which all the day's activities took place. The walls were hung with tapestry or curtaining and there were benches fixed along the sides, sufficiently wide for a man to sleep on at night. The floor was paved, and there were double doors at one end, large enough to allow a horse to enter. There were trestle-tables, which could be stacked up when not in use, and a great open fire burning in the middle of the room. By day the hall was a litter of hunting equipment, of weapons and harness and alive with servants, wolfhounds and even hawks. ("No good hawk flies through the hall, nor does the swift horse stamp in the courtyard", says the poem *Beowulf* of a deserted hall.) Kitchens and the royal quarters were usually separate, but the great hall would be the place where even a prince spent most of his day-to-day life when he was not out in the open.

The costume of a thane or a prince consisted of heavy underclothes and, above these, trousers cross-gartered to the knee. He wore soft shoes, and the upper part of the body was covered by a knee-length tunic, caught in with a belt at the waist. The belt carried a knife and a pouch, for there were no pockets. On ceremonial occasions there would be a sword as well. Out of doors the nobleman would also wear a cloak caught up on the left shoulder with a heavy brooch. The general effect was rather that of an eighteenth-century highlander.

Asser might complain that Alfred was still illiterate at the age of twelve, but this was really beside the point for a great part of a nobleman's education took place in the open air, when he was learning to hunt, to track a wild boar, or tame a hawk. Sir John Spelman, in his seventeenth-century life of Alfred comments:

> The *Saxons* (from their *German* ancestors) holding Hunting a most generous and laudable Education of youth, as that which inured them to Hardiness, made them active, patient of Labour, and acquainted with Danger. . . .

The complex lore of hunting took the place of climbing, organized games and biology today. There was a great deal more to it than just going into a forest and throwing a spear at a wild animal.

After sunset the household, tired from a day spent in the open, feasted in the hall (especially in the long winter evenings) drinking mead, ale or wine. Professional minstrels, attached to the court, or wandering from settlement to settlement, played the harp and recited long poems, half-history, half fairy-story. The most complete example that now exists is *Beowulf*, a poem of just over three thousand lines, dealing with the Saxons' ancestors in Denmark and with the monster Grendel and his mother:

> Wild and lonely the land they live in,
> Wind-swept ridges and wolf-retreats,
> Dread tracts of fen where the falling torrent
> Downward dips into gloom and shadow,
> Under the dusk of the darkening cliff. . . .

For twelve years the king of Denmark's life has been made intolerable by this mist-monster Grendel. Often, angry at the sound of the harp-music, Grendel comes and kills the retainers. Soon the great hall stands empty. (It is a hall like the one the audience are sitting in.) Beowulf hears of this and comes from Sweden to offer his services to the Danish king. A bench is cleared in the hall and there is laughter and noise. The queen and her daughter hand mead to each in order of precedence, the provision of hospitality being, for the Saxons, a woman's most important duty. Another poem, *Judith*, describes the ideal queen as follows:

> A woman shall prosper, be loved among her people, shall be cheerful, keep counsel, be liberal with horses and treasure, always, everywhere, greet first at the mead-drinking the protector of nobles before the band of retainers, give the first cup promptly into her lord's hand, and study the benefit of them both in her housekeeping.

After the feast Beowulf and his men sleep in the hall. Grendel enters and fights with Beowulf. Benches inlaid with gold are hurled about. It is surprising—the poem says—that the hall itself did not collapse, but fortunately it was braced inside and outside with iron clamps. In the end, Beowulf tears off Grendel's arm, and the monster runs away, to die in the fen out of which he had come.

There is a celebration feast in the damaged hall, now hung with golden tapestries, and the harp is struck "and many ballads recited". Later, benches are pushed away and bedding spread on the floor; but that night Grendel's mother takes her revenge for the death of her son, carrying off the king's favourite counsellor.

Beowulf comes to the rescue once more, tracks Grendel's mother to an underwater cave and there kills her. Having returned in triumph there is a third feast and much giving of presents. Next day Beowulf and his followers sail for home.

The second half of the poem describes how fifty years later, Beowulf, now a king, kills a dragon that is ravaging his own country, but himself dies of his wounds. His body is burned and its ashes buried in a great barrow, a mound of earth, with gold collars and brooches.

So those who had shared his hall "said that of all kings he was the gentlest and most gracious of men, the kindest to his people and the most desirous of renown".

In Alfred's day kings were no longer buried like Beowulf since the Saxons had become Christians. Other contemporary poems have survived, of a religious nature. The most moving is the *Dream of the Rood*, which describes the thoughts of the Cross:

> Long years ago (well yet I remember)
> They hewed me down on the edge of the holt,
> Severed my trunk; strong foemen took me,
> For a spectacle wrought me, a gallows for rogues.

It was easy for Christian faith and pagan legend to live comfortably side by side in people's minds; the world of Grendel co-existed with that of the Holy Rood. One could look out from the churches of Wessex to the high bare downs where there were white horses, barrows, megaliths, and the strange stone circles of Stonehenge, Avebury and Stanton Drew. They were there when the Saxons came, and it was clear that they were the homes of monsters and magic.

Alfred, listening wide-eyed to the poems, could see in the flickering torchlight a hall just like the one in which Beowulf feasted and fought. And outside not far from his birthplace at Wantage, there was "Weland's Smithy"—to us a Neolithic long barrow, but to the Saxons the home of a magic blacksmith. Tether your horse there, leaving a silver penny on the capstone, and when you came back the money would be gone and your horse new-shod. Years later Alfred referred to him in his translation of Boethius as "the famous and wise goldsmith Weland". It was easy to believe in the magic outside the Christian security of the hall. Was not one of Alfred's own ancestors called *Sceaf*, the Sheaf, a corn-king who had floated alone in a mysterious boat to the island of Britain?

Hunting by day and legends by night; that perhaps had been the basic warp and woof of Alfred's childhood. But now he was sixteen and a man, second-in-command in the kingdom of Wessex, and as messengers came spurring to his brother's court with the news that a Danish Great Army was occupying the

kingdom of East Anglia, Alfred had for the first time to share
the responsibility of government.

The news was more momentous than King Ethelred and his
young second-in-command could possibly realize. It heralded a
generation of warfare and the permanent occupation by the
foreigner of half of England. It was to prove as decisive a landing as that of the Normans almost exactly two hundred years
later.

Yet for one person who has heard of the Danish descent on the
land in the summer of 866, hundreds have at least a nodding ac-
quaintance with "1066 and all that". There are several reasons
why this should be so; the Danish conquest was over-shadowed
by the Norman one simply because the latter came later in time
and was the last successful invasion of these islands. Then, too,
the Danish conquest was a long drawn-out affair of decades and
therefore lacks the close-knit drama of Harold's nine-months'
reign. For the Norman Conquest there is the Bayeux Tapestry to
set the imagination working, and plenty of written sources as
well; but the Danes were a destructive army on the move, un-
concerned with written records. The facts of the lengthy struggle
have to be inferred from the brief entries—often ambiguous—in
the *Anglo-Saxon Chronicle*. And the *Chronicle* is naturally even
less informative about the Danish victories.

For the Danish leaders, Halfdan and Ivar the Boneless, the problem was where to strike first. To meet their threat stood five kingdoms—in theory. But in fact it must have seemed to the Danes
that none would put up a very strong resistance. Northumbria
was torn by royal feuds. East Anglia was small and pitifully exposed to the North Sea. Mercia had played no decisive part in the
affairs of England for fifty years. Wessex had declined since the
great days of Egbert, and was ruled by a young and untried
king.

The first thing to do was to acquire a base in the island. For that
purpose East Anglia possessed many advantages. It was easily
accessible by sea and river. It was protected from any possible
Saxon counter-attack by forests to the south and fens to the east.
(Not that it seemed very likely that one Saxon kingdom would
come to the help of another.) Having occupied East Anglia the
Danes would keep the strategic initiative. They would hold the

interior lines of communication and from this base would be able to strike north towards Northumbria, inland due west against Mercia, or south-west into Wessex, taking whatever direction pleased them best.

Edmund, the young king of East Anglia, came to terms with the heathen quickly. The *Chronicle*, it will be remembered, recorded that

> ... the Great Army came to the land of the English and took up their winter quarters in East Anglia—and there they were supplied with horses, and the men of East Anglia made peace with them ...

The Danes spent a year in the east and then, in the autumn of 867, they rode out of East Anglia on their borrowed horses. To Alfred and his brother, watching events closely, it must have appeared that the East Anglians had bought off the invader cheaply—but in the near future there lay conquest for the people and martyrdom for King Edmund.

For the time being, however, the Danes moved north. Wessex could breathe again as the news came that the Vikings were riding up the paved road to the north, the remains of the Roman Ermine Street, the only direct link between the kingdom of Northumbria and the south. The Great Army passed through Lincoln and crossed the estuary of the Humber by boat. On All Saints' Day it broke through the ruined Roman walls into York and made that city its new base.

The Danish strategy was one that they repeated often in later years. The elements of it were simple and usually brought success. A surprise landing would be made, often at some point on a river well inland from the coast; the Danes would then throw up an encampment and from these temporary walls sally out to round up horses. These were not used as cavalry in battles, but as transport rather in the manner of seventeenth-century dragoons. When they felt strong and mobile enough, the Danes would seize a town and use this as a permanent base. From its security they could conduct further lightning raids, store plunder, and lay up for the winter.

Using York for this purpose the Great Army ravaged the countryside to the north as far as the River Tyne "and filled every place with bloodshed and sorrow", as Simeon of Durham later

wrote. Where they had been they left nothing behind but the
roofless walls of churches and monasteries. Then they withdrew
to York to winter there and wait for the reaction of the rulers of
Northumbria.

The Danes had so far met with no resistance in the north because the Northumbrians had, as usual, been fighting a private
war among themselves. King Osbert had been expelled and replaced by a usurper, Ælle. Legend has clustered round these men.
One story, as has been seen, credits Ælle with the death of the
Viking Ragnar Lothbrok and sees the Danish invasion as moti-
vated by vengeance. Another story says that Osbert had raped the
wife of one of his chief nobles while the man was down at the
coast watching for pirates. In this version it is the aggrieved noble
who invites the Danes to Northumbria.

Whatever the truth of the matter, Northumbria was certainly
torn by dissension and in no state to take on the invader. At last,
too late, the rival kings united their forces and marched against
the Danes in York. On 21st March the Danish army withdrew
within the walls. The Northumbrians, thinking that this was the
moment of victory, rushed on "and," says the *Chronicle*, "some
of them got within the town and there was an immense slaughter
made of the Northumbrians—some within, others without; and
both the kings were slain; and the survivors made peace with the
Great Army."

A feigned retreat was a common tactical device of the Danes
and Normans—it was used with great success at the battle of
Hastings—and it sounds as though the Northumbrians blundered
into a pre-arranged trap. At all events the fighting on that spring
day at York marked the end after three hundred years of the
power of Northumbria, once the most civilized state in England.
"No other battle in the north of England ever produced so great a
cataclysm. . . . In the battle of York a dynasty was broken, a religion half-smothered, and a culture was barbarized."

Now there were three kingdoms left: East Anglia, Mercia and
Wessex. In the autumn of 868 the Great Army placed a Saxon
puppet ruler, Egbert, on the Northumbrian throne, evacuated its
base at York, having taken what it could from that area, and
moved south into Mercia, where it set up winter quarters at
Nottingham. As always, the Danish choice for a base was

geographically excellent. Nottingham was near enough to York-shire for them to keep an eye on the subdued peoples there, while the town itself stood near the Fosse Way, the Roman main road running diagonally from Chester to London. It also controlled the route down the Trent to the North Sea.

Burhred, the king of Mercia, had married Alfred's sister Æthels-with. Now he sent urgent messengers riding posthaste to his brothers-in-law in Wessex. There King Ethelred and Alfred (now about nineteen years old) gathered the army of Wessex and hurried north to the assistance of Mercia. The combined armies approached Nottingham and faced the Danes, safe inside the earthworks which they had as usual thrown up. "But," says the *Chronicle*, "no heavy fighting took place there, and the Mercians made peace with the Great Army." Perhaps Burhred, remembering what had happened to the Northumbrians when they had attempted to storm the Danish defences at York, decided that discretion was the better part of valour. The army of Wessex had apparently come a long way for nothing. Can one detect in the Chronicler's comment a faint note of disgust and disappointment at the apparent anti-climax?

In fact the abortive encounter at Nottingham was not quite so indecisive as it appeared at first sight to be, since it had the effect of causing the Danes to put off for the time being their intended assault on Mercia. Instead they retired for a whole year to Northumbria, spending a second winter at York. No doubt Alfred, whose career shows that he learnt rapidly by experience, drew the obvious conclusion: resist the Danes, and they would go where plunder could be more easily got.

It was during this year that Alfred married Ealhswith, a Mercian noblewoman, the daughter of an ealdorman and related on her mother's side to the royal house of Mercia. The union was clearly intended to cement the alliance between the two Saxon kingdoms, but there is no evidence to show whether it took place before or after the encounter with the Danes at Nottingham, though common-sense suggests that it would not be celebrated until after the Danish threat had been removed.

The wedding festivities were marred by a mysterious and, to contemporaries, ominous disaster. Asser's biography describes the event in infuriatingly vague terms:

After Alfred's wedding had been celebrated in Mercia in the presence of a countless multitude of people of both sexes, and after continual feasting day and night, Alfred was suddenly seized—in the presence of all the people—by an overwhelming pain, unknown to all the physicians. Those who were then present, and those who have seen him daily since that time, were equally ignorant of its origin. And unfortunately the worst feature of it is that it should have continued incessantly during so many years, from the twentieth to past the fortieth year of his life.

The nature of Alfred's illness remains unknown. In another part of his *Life* Asser says that Alfred "has been constantly attacked by an unknown complaint, so that he has not a moment's ease—either he suffers the pain which it causes, or he suffers from the gloom which is thrown over him by the fear of its coming." Two points are made. Whatever happened at the wedding, when Asser was at court and Alfred was about forty, the king was ill. Secondly, the nature of the illness was painful, incurable, and intermittent.

So much is clear. The rest can only be guesswork. Later stories elaborated Alfred's illnesses. It was said that he suffered from the *ficus*—interpreted as piles—when a boy, that when hunting in Cornwall he prayed at the shrine of St. Neot that he might receive a lighter affliction, and that in consequence the *ficus* was healed and replaced by this new infirmity at the time of his marriage.

Medical science, of course, was rudimentary—except among the pagan Arabs. Contemporary remedies for piles included the roots of burdock, heated, worked into a plaster, and applied. Or one might take celandine roots, holding the stem while one repeated nine Paternosters and at the ninth "deliver us from evil" uprooting the plant, soaking the roots and applying them by a hot fire. Both these remedies were very ancient—how ancient is shown by the fact that in neither case must the roots be touched by iron. "Cold iron" was said to drive away spirits and the origin of this belief—and consequently of the prohibition—must date back to the first arrival of the magic metal in Britain, a thousand years before the days of Alfred.

The onset of a new disease at the time of Alfred's marriage suggests to a modern mind that the disease was not purely physical but rather what would at present be called psychosomatic—the mind working on the body to produce physical symptoms. Contemporary observers often attributed disease to "the evil eye" or "the envy of the devil"—essentially psychological explanations in medieval terms.

Nineteenth-century lives of Alfred tend to settle for piles as a disease of his youth, and for either epilepsy or the stone as the disease that came on him at his marriage. Epilepsy seems unlikely, since the symptoms were known to Anglo-Saxon medicine and would have been recognized, but the stone could account for the intermittent nature of the pain.

Finally, there is in Asser's *Life* a sentence to the effect that Alfred "had great dread of leprosy or blindness, or any such complaint as makes men useless or contemptible when it afflicts them". If "great dread" is used accurately it brings one back once more to the possibility that the illness was rooted in Alfred's mind rather than his body.

As has been said already, no conclusion is possible, but the various suggested explanations are worth considering since they all in their different ways hint at a weaker, more imaginative, side of Alfred's mental make-up often ignored in the contemporary picture of a strong man.

In the autumn King Ethelred and Alfred rode south to winter in the royal palaces of Wessex, no doubt debating in what direction the Danes would be likely to move next spring. Would they strike at Mercia again, or would they ride for Wessex and revenge?

In the event, the Great Army did neither of these things but moved instead south and east across a corner of Mercia back into East Anglia—to the kingdom that had failed to resist them when they first landed.

The previous year had been a lean one for them, so now they took a double toll. The Great Army left a trail of devastation in its wake, sacking monasteries "once full rich but now brought to naught" as a chronicler lamented. Bardeny and Crowland, Ely and Medeshamsted (Peterborough)—the flames roared into the summer skies from one after another of the great abbeys. Ingulf's account of what happened at Crowland, though written later, contains circumstantial details which he was unlikely to have invented:

When news of the Great Army's approach reached the abbot of Crowland he sent away all the able-bodied men. They took with them the monastery's relics, including the body of their founder St. Guthlac, his scourge and his psalter. All these they hid in the nearest fen. Then they collected the chalices and precious plate and lowered them down the well that stood in the cloister yard.

Next they took the great gold-encrusted altarpiece, the gift of a king, and threw that into the well, but an unforeseen complication was now met with.

The end of the altarpiece, on account of its length, always appeared above the water, and therefore (as they perceived the fires from the towns in Kesteven approaching nearer and nearer, and fearing lest the Pagans should come upon them suddenly) they drew it out and left it with the abbot and elder monks.

These hid the intractable altarpiece outside the church on the north side. Then the abbot put on his vestments and, with the old men and boys who were left, "kept regular hours of service"— and waited.

As Mass was ending the Danes burst into the monastery and hunted the remaining monks through the maze of abbey buildings. The abbot was cut down in the vestry, the sub-prior in the refectory. When there was no one left alive except one boy whom they spared because of his beauty, the Danes looked for their winnings. They searched high and low, even breaking open the tombs, "and when they did not find the expected treasures, they were filled with indignation and, piling up in the most pitiable manner the whole body of the saints into one heap, they set fire to them . . . together with the church and all the buildings."

The sack of Crowland took place on 26th August. Similar scenes occurred at Peterborough a few days later. Then the Great Army moved on to Thetford, on the borders of Norfolk and Suffolk, and prepared to take up winter quarters there. Edmund, the young king of East Anglia, led his army against them. What followed next is recounted briefly in the *Chronicle* as follows:

King Edmund fought with them and the Danes gained the victory and slew the king and subdued all that land.

That is, so to speak, the official record. Yet within half a century of his death Edmund was widely honoured in what had once been his kingdom as a saint, and Sir Frank Stenton, the authority on this period, writes, "the early development of his cult suggests very strongly that a basis of fact underlay the legend of his martyrdom".

It is worth listening, therefore, to the story that a Frankish monk, Abbo, set down not more than a century after Edmund's death. He had heard the details, he said, from St. Dunstan of Canterbury, who had been told them by a very old man, once King Edmund's sword-bearer. This was the story:

The king was at his royal manor at Hoxne, on the River Waveney, when a horseman rode up with a message from the Viking leader, Ivar the Boneless. He demanded briefly that Edmund should become his vassal. The king refused. No Christian, he said, should take a pagan as his lord. The messenger carrying his reply met the Danish vanguard, already close at hand. The enraged Danes pushed rapidly on and seized Edmund as he was preparing to leave, but they did not recognize the king.

"Where is Edmund? Tell us."

The king replied in one of those riddling sentences the Saxons loved.

"I will do so, willingly and at once. Before I prepared to leave, Edmund was here and I with him; when I turned to go, he did the same; I do not know if he will be able to escape you, for now the fate of the king is in the hands of God, and of Jesus, who is his Lord."

The vanguard seized this ambiguous young man and held him a prisoner until Ivar the Boneless arrived with the main body of men. They, of course, recognized the man with whom they had had dealings when they first landed in England five years before. Let the chronicler Gaimar finish the tale.

What then did these enemies? They caused him to be tied to a tree. Then they told him that he should be tormented with a strange death. They sent for their archers; they shot at the king with handbows. They shot so frequently and pierced him so much, that his body was stuck as full of the darts which these villains shot, as the skin of a hedgehog is thick with sharp prickles when he carries apples from the orchard . . .

One thinks of Red Indians whooping round the stake of a tortured captive.

> To this hour, I believe, they might have shot before the king would have done anything which these men wished. Then they sent a wicked man, whose name was Coran Colbe, to cut off the head of the saint. So was Edmund killed as a martyr.

When the Danes had left Hoxne, the king's men came cautiously back. They found the king's body, but not his head. As they searched, a voice called, "Here! Here!" They followed the sound and came on a huge wolf, which was guarding the head between its paws. The wolf padded quietly after them as they carried the head back to the king's manor—and then disappeared from the story.

For thirty-three years King Edmund's body remained at Hoxne. Then it was transferred to Bædriceswirde—the name of the settlement which eventually grew to be known as Bury St. Edmunds. A rich abbey grew up beside Edmund's shrine, and the 20th November became his feast day. Edmund's fame spread throughout England: there are still more than sixty churches dedicated to him. At Hoxne (pronounced *hoxen*) a great oak, said to be St. Edmund's, stood alone in the fields until it fell down in the middle of the last century. Today a rather unsatisfactory marble cross marks the spot, but at Hengrave Hall nearby there is a piece of oak that once lay in Hoxne church—and there is an arrow embedded in it.

England gained a martyr, but lost a kingdom. It was the end of East Anglia. After Edmund's death the Vikings "subdued the whole of that kingdom". Northumbria was gone, East Anglia was gone. Now there were only two independent states left: Mercia and Wessex. Which of them, King Ethelred and Alfred must have wondered, would be next for the Danish chopping-block?

The Year of Battles (871)

... he rode along the line and gave advice and showed his
warriors how they should stand steady, ordered them to
hold their shields properly, firm in their hands, and not be
afraid.

The Battle of Maldon, 991

THE Danes lived for a year off the fat of East Anglia. Then the
Great Army moved again. Its leaders chose to go south-west
into Wessex. It was, as usual, a sensible choice. Mercia, lying
away from the sea, was for the Vikings the most inaccessible of
the Saxon kingdoms. Those parts that they could most easily
reach, in the north and east, had been recently plundered. Better
to let them lie fallow for a bit. Wessex, on the other hand, had
lain untouched for years. The Icknield ridgeway from Danish-
held East Anglia would lead their forces easily straight into the
heart of the kingdom. Now was the time to probe its defences
and test the determination of its King Ethelred. Perhaps he would
not wish to risk martyrdom!

The Great Army, then, rode along the Chilterns, swept through
the Goring Gap, and by the coming of winter had dug itself in at
Reading. As always, the Vikings were already installed in their
new base before people had grasped that they were on the move
again.

Ivar the Boneless was no longer in command—he had gone to
Ireland, where he ruled the Vikings there until his death about
three years later. His brother, Halfdan, now led the Army; he
took up a strong position between the Kennet and the Thames,
a typical Danish encampment based on a town and with good
natural defences—in this case, water on three sides.

The Danes at once set to work to throw up an embankment on
the fourth, exposed, side of their position. While they were

digging themselves in they sent out foraging parties into the surrounding Berkshire countryside. It was about Christmas that one
of these parties under a *jarl* (chief, or "earl") called Sidroc was
unfortunate enough to run accidentally into a band of Saxons led
by Ethelwulf, ealdorman of Berkshire, at Englefield four or five
miles from their base camp. This was the same Ethelwulf who had
defeated the Danes when they stormed Winchester ten years
before.

Neither group was expecting to meet the other, and one can
imagine the momentary pause of surprise before the swords
came out. In the ensuing skirmish Sidroc and his party were
routed. This fortuitous clash was the beginning of the great
struggle for Wessex—and the Saxons had drawn first blood.

Four days after the Englefield incident King Ethelred and his
brother Alfred reached the area with the main Saxon army. They
attacked the Danish earthworks and, as so often happened when
the Saxons attempted to take a prepared position, were repulsed.
Ethelwulf, victorious only four days before, was killed in the
mêlée. His body was recovered and buried at Derby in Mercia
(He was probably by birth a Mercian, for Berkshire had once been
part of Mercia and Ethelwulf had been granted an estate at Pang-
bourne in the days before it became part of Wessex.)

The score, one might say, was now one all, but neither Englefield nor Reading were full-scale battles.

The first real test of strength came on the 8th January 871, a
"Ashdown", somewhere on the northern slope of the Berkshire
Downs. It is impossible, as so often in those days, to be certain of
the site of this battle, in which Alfred was to play a decisive part.
The whole length of the Downs was then known as "Ashdown".
Popular sentiment has placed the battle near the White Horse of
Uffington, at the western end of the ridge. Eighteenth-century
archaeologists took the beautifully simplified Horse to be Alfred's
memorial to the victory: but in fact this 360-foot figure—the
oldest "white horse" in the country—was apparently cut in the
first century B.C. Uffington, moreover, is thirty miles from
Reading as the crow flies, and it is unlikely the battle would have
taken place so far from the Danes' base. Modern opinion inclines
to place the site at the eastern end of the Berkshire ridge. Lieutenant-Colonel Burne, in his *More Battlefields of England*, has argued

that the most probable area lies on the Ridgeway near this eastern end. He places it a dozen miles or so to the north-west of Reading, just beyond Streatley, and close to the earthwork of Lowbury Hill, which in that case would have been the Saxon assembly point.

The Danish army left the security of their encampment at Reading a few days after they had thrown back the Saxon attack. They may have meant to pick up supplies for the winter from the rich farmland of the Vale of the White Horse to the north, or they may have intended all along to seek a battle with the recently-defeated Saxons. A third possibility is that they sought to strike into the interior of Wessex and eventually transfer their headquarters from Reading to the interior of the kingdom.

Two lines of advance offered themselves. From Reading the Danes could climb to the crest of the Downland and move west along the Ridgeway which would lead them eventually to Chippenham. Or they could wheel south from the ridge to the deserted Roman town of Silchester and follow the old road that ran from there south to Winchester. Whichever plan the Danes intended to adopt it involved the movement of the entire army under its two "kings" and numerous jarls.

The Saxons, meanwhile, had not dispersed after their unsuccessful attack on Reading. King Ethelred and Alfred had kept the fyrd—the Saxon militia—together and were watching the Danish movements closely. As soon as the Danes left the shelter of their encampment the Saxons moved also. They allowed the Danes to get just too far from Reading to turn back. Before revealing themselves they probably marched west through the Vale of the White Horse for 10 or 12 miles, parallel to the Danish army on the heights. Battle was joined just beyond Streatley.

According to Asser—and one must remember that he claims to have obtained his information from eye-witnesses—the Danish army was formed up on the higher ground in two divisions. One part was commanded by the two kings, Halfdan (Ragnar's son) and Bacsecg, the other by the lesser jarls. (Another reading, from a military point of view more satisfactory, would place the kings in the centre, and the forces of the jarls on each flank, but this will not make sense of the Saxon dispositions.)

Seeing this, the Saxons adopted a similar plan of battle, dividing

their army into two parts as well. Ethelred's forces faced those of
the kings, Alfred's those of the jarls. This is how Asser describes
the preparations for the battle:

> The Christians encountered the pagan army at a place called Ash-
> down. The pagans had divided themselves into two bodies and made
> two shield-walls of equal strength. Since they had two kings and
> many jarls, they gave one part of the army to the two kings, and the
> other to the jarls. The Christians, seeing this, divided their army also
> into two equal parts, and immediately formed their shield-walls.
> ... Now the Christians had decided that King Ethelred with his men
> should attack the two pagan kings, and his brother Alfred, with his
> men, should take the chance of battle against the jarls.

Although the Vikings were professionals, as one might say,
and the Saxons amateurs, the two armies would look very similar.
Both sides wore tunics caught in at the waist by the sword-belt,
and cross-gartered hose. The heavy cloaks would have been
thrown aside, or, if the weather was very cold, worn tied back to
leave both arms free for the fight. The Saxon rank-and-file carried a cutlass (*scramasax*), a light one-handed axe, and a spear. This
last had a shaft of ash about 6 ft. long and an iron blade.

The professional bodyguards of the Saxon thanes were more
heavily armoured. They wore a round metal head-piece and a
shirt of chain-mail, and carried a straight-edged long-sword together with a round shield about 2 ft. in diameter, backed with
wood and faced with ox-hide. (Sometimes sheepskin, a very inferior substitute, was used instead. Alfred's grandson, Athelstan,
had to pass a law forbidding this practice.)

The Danes had much the same equipment. Their long-swords
were of a rather better pattern with a heavy pommel to balance
the blade, a more efficient guard, and a blade that tapered to a
point—an improved model which the Saxons soon began to
imitate. In addition, the Danish axes were much heavier and
longer, requiring two hands if they were to be used effectively.
Their army was probably more colourful too. They tended to
wear gayer clothes than the Saxons, they painted their shields, and
they carried their plunder with them in the shape of gold trap-
pings and heavy gold arm bands.

The rival armies made their "shield-wall" by forming up their men so that the shield of each man in the front row overlapped that of the man to his left. Then the two armies waited to see which would make the first move. An important preliminary was the shouting of battle-cries, battle-songs and insults intended to alarm the opposition or provoke them to attack first. The light glittered from gold and silver bracelets and shaken weapons. Above the armies flags were shaken, and over all hung on the one side the Viking raven and on the other the golden dragon of Wessex.

Asser describes what happened next:

> Alfred, as we have been told by truthful eye-witnesses, marched up more quickly than his brother; for King Ethelred was still in his tent, praying and hearing Mass, and he declared he would not leave it until the priest had finished, nor leave Divine service for the service of men. . . .

> The king remained long in prayer, and the pagans came up quickly, ready to fight. Then Alfred, second in command, could bear the attacks of the enemy no longer. He must either retreat, or begin the battle without waiting for his brother. At last he led his forces like a wild boar against the enemy, without waiting for his brother's arrival. . . .

> The pagans held the higher ground, and the Christians came up from below. There was in that place a single stunted thorn tree, which we have ourselves seen. At this point the opposing armies met, with loud shouts on both sides—one side fighting for evil ends, the other for their lives, their loved ones, and their country. And when both armies had fought long and bravely, at last the pagans . . . having lost the greater part of their army, fled.

One of the two kings, Bacsecg, five jarls, and thousands of men were slain on the Danish side, "covering with their bodies the whole breadth of Ashdown" as the Saxons pursued them through the night back to their base at Reading.

This, then, is the description of Alfred's first victory as Asser had it from the mouths of survivors, including presumably the king himself. What stands out is Alfred's initiative in ordering the advance when it became clear to him that it would be fatal to wait for Ethelred to finish his prayers. (Asser implies that these prayers nevertheless played their part in assuring the Saxons of victory.) What is not clear is whether Alfred ordered the king's division to advance as well as his own, but it seems reasonable to assume that he did.

If Lieutenant-Colonel Burne is correct in his identification of the site of the battle, the local names "Awful Bottom" and "Dead Man's Hollow" for the dry valley which lies across the line of Alfred's advance acquire an added significance. In Domesday Book the name of this Hundred is "Nachededorn"—Naked Thorn, which powerfully suggests the single, stumpy thorn that Asser saw for himself.

Of the results of Ashdown, the point has frequently been made that few decisive victories have yielded such disappointing immediate fruits.

Spelman writing three centuries ago called Ashdown "rather a presage of Alfred's future success than any real Progress of the present Affairs". And yet Ashdown was "a famous victory". Although within a fortnight the Danes were pillaging the heart of Wessex, yet nevertheless the Saxons had shown that the Danes could be held and beaten by a Saxon army—and this demonstration owed its success largely to Alfred's prompt if impetuous action in the opening stages of the struggle. It was the first but not the last time that the king was powerfully to affect the course of events.

Meanwhile after Ashdown the Danes withdrew to their base at Reading, from which they launched raids far into the territory of Wessex. Reading was a good centre for this sort of warfare and during the year 871 the Danes moved out along first one and then another of the routes from Reading—west along the Berkshire ridgeway towards Chippenham, south-west along the Roman Port Way to Salisbury, south to Winchester and Southampton. Each time they were opposed by the army of Wessex, but each time too as the year wore on they cut deeper and deeper into the heartland of the Saxon kingdom.

Less than fourteen days after their defeat by Alfred and his brother at Ashdown, the Danes had broken out of their camp at Reading, where the Saxons thought they had them securely penned, and moved south along the Winchester road. They were located by the Saxons at Old Basing, near Basingstoke.

The Danish position, as usual, was a good defensive one, being protected by the water-meadows of the River Loddon. On 22nd

January an attempt by King Ethelred and Alfred to storm the camp failed and the Saxons drew off to lick their wounds. Nevertheless the Danish raid in that direction had been checked.

After so much fighting—there had been four encounters in the space of a month—there appears to have been a lull. At all events, nothing further is recorded until two months later. It is likely that the Saxon national levy was temporarily disbanded. One of the problems with which Alfred was later to grapple was that of keeping an army in the field for long periods, particularly if it had won a victory. There was a natural tendency for the thegns to go home to their districts with their levies to find out what was happening there. In addition, it was difficult to keep the army supplied for long. The Danes did not have these problems—they had no homes to worry about, and no supply problems to consider, since they lived off the countryside.

On 22nd March the king and Alfred met the enemy in another pitched battle. This took place at "Meretun", probably the modern village of Marten, eight miles south-east of Marlborough, at a point where the track running west across Salisbury Plain from Basingstoke was intersected by a former Roman road from Marlborough to Winchester. If this is the right place, it represented a march of thirty miles or so from Reading—a deeper penetration by the Danes into Wessex than any they had yet accomplished.

So far the Saxon fyrd had a little more than held its own: it had failed to drive the Danes from their fortified base, but it had on the whole contained them, and it had won the one pitched battle, at Ashdown. Now the fortune turned.

The Danish army was drawn up, as at Ashdown, in two parts. There was fierce fighting through the day. At first the Danes gave way and the Saxons "for long in the day were victorious". But as the short afternoon faded into evening the Danes counterattacked and drove the Saxons from the field. Perhaps their earlier flight had been one of those feints of which they were so fond, or perhaps they merely lasted out better than their opponents. Whatever the reason for their success, it was a black hour for Wessex, cancelling the earlier success at Ashdown. The Danish army had marched far into Wessex, from the field of battle they could now strike at Chippenham, Salisbury or Winchester. Heahmund, one

of the fighting bishops of Sherborne and an old and trusted adviser, had been killed in the struggle. (His death helps to fix the
exact date of the battle, since he was later regarded in England as
a saint, and 22nd March was his feast day.)

There was worse to follow.

Immediately after the defeat at Meretun messengers from the
London area stumbled into the king's presence with the news
that a fresh force had arrived from overseas and had made its
way safely to the Danish base at Reading—"a summer army in-
numerable," they reported, "eager to fight against the army of
Wessex."

This disastrous information had hardly been received when a
third blow struck the kingdom. From court horsemen rode hard
to the local thegns with the news that the king was dead.

King Ethelred, the third and last of Alfred's brothers, had died
soon after Easter, which fell on 15th April that year. Unlike his
brothers, who lie at Sherborne, he was buried on the outskirts of
the New Forest at Wimborne Minster, a few miles to the north of
Bournemouth. A seventeenth-century inscription at Wimborne
reads, "St. Ethelred the Martyr, King of the West Saxons, who
fell by the hands of the heathen Danes". There is no contemporary
account of how he met his death. Perhaps he had been wounded at
Meretun—which would help to explain why the Saxons lost
heart in the afternoon—and died of his wounds a few weeks later.

The situation could hardly have been worse: the Saxons defeated; a fresh Danish army arrived and hot for plunder; the king
dead, leaving behind two little boys far too young to rule. All
now depended on the king's former second-in-command,
Alfred.

The Critical Years (871–8)

... they were become a mighty army, like Locusts covering the Face of the Earth, they despise any longer to be resisted by so poor an handfull as the *Saxons* now were grown into, and therefore, contrary to Faith, and Oath, and the security of their Hostages, they enter the King's Country, and, like a raging floud, bearing all before it, they chace away the Natives.

Sir John Spelman, 1643

THE late king had left two sons, Ethelwold and Ethelhelm, but Alfred was the only man of the royal house who might face the Danes, and that—remembering the fate of St. Edmund—was not an especially desirable position in which to be. The king's council, the witan, at once recognized Alfred as his brother's successor, a position which, Asser wrote later, Alfred accepted reluctantly. There was only honour and danger in it. Sir John Spelman comments dryly:

> So at the best, it was rather an Entertainment of a Title, than an Acceptance of a Crown. . . . The King's Hand was now at the Plough, and his Fortunes lay upon it, there was no looking back, neither was there any Difficulty in what he had to chose. He had only to hazard whether he would be overthrown or devoured. . . .

And so Alfred became king of Wessex "with the full consent of all the inhabitants of the kingdom". If there was anything in the nature of a coronation ceremony it must have been a hasty, huddled affair, for there was hard fighting to be done. No time must be wasted. Even while Alfred was mourning at Wimborne, news came that the Saxons had been defeated in another attack on the Danish position at Reading. Perhaps later in the year there was a formal coronation, but on the other hand it is possible that the ceremony may not have taken place for years. Alfred's descendant Edgar came to the throne in 959, but was not crowned until 973, when he had reached the age of thirty. This was the minimum canonical age for ordination as a priest, and the king's office was regarded as in some ways of a similar sanctity. This consideration may have delayed Alfred's coronation for some years.

There is no evidence, one way or the other. Much later the monks of Westminster claimed that Alfred was crowned there with the crown the Pope had used when he was a little boy in Rome, but this was only an attempt to establish their claim that they had always crowned the kings of England. They had indeed in their possession a very old crown, used at the coronation service, but it probably did not date back beyond the eleventh century and the reign of Edward the Confessor. Of this so-called "crown of king Alfred" Spelman wrote:

> . . . in the arched Room in the Cloisters of *Westminster* Abbey, where the ancient *Regalia* of this Kingdom are kept, upon a Box (which is the Cabinet to the ancientest Crown) there is (as I am informed) an Inscription to this purpose . . . "Here is Alfred's crown". And the Crown (which to this purpose were worth the Observing) is of a very ancient Work, with Flowers adorned with Stones of somewhat a plain Setting . . .

This crown was destroyed at the time of the Commonwealth.

We have not got Alfred's crown, and we do not know when or where the coronation took place, but we can make a reasonable guess as to the form the service took, for there exists an eye-witness account of the coronation of Alfred's great-grandson Edgar, a hundred years later. It is an elaborate ritual and if it developed gradually much must have been in existence in Alfred's day. Essentially, it is the form of service still used today, a thousand years later.

The king, robed and crowned, was led into the church by two bishops. He took off his crown and prostrated himself before the altar while the *Te Deum* was sung. Then the bishops raised the king and he gave his promise (*promissio*) to rule justly:

"In the name of the Holy Trinity. I promise three things to the Christian people subject to me. First that God's church and all Christian people of my dominions shall keep true peace. Secondly, that I forbid to all ranks robbery and all injustice. Thirdly, that I promise justice and mercy in all judgements, that the gracious and compassionate God, who liveth and reigneth, may through that grant us his eternal mercy."

After this promise to preserve peace and order and to rule justly, the king was anointed to the sounds of *Vivat rex in aeternum.* The archbishop put a ring on his finger, a sword at his waist and a crown on his head. After the blessing, Mass was celebrated. In the evening, after the service, there was a coronation feast.

Whatever hasty ceremonies may have followed immediately after his brother's funeral, Alfred was soon involved in defence of his kingdom. Within a month the Danes had penetrated farther into Wessex than ever before. They clashed with Alfred at the royal manor of Wilton, about four miles west of Salisbury. The *Chronicle* recounts how the new King with a small band fought against the Danish army and for the greater part of the day held them off; but once more the Danes feigned flight and then, Asser says, "deceived their over-optimistic pursuers, rallied, and gained the victory."

There were other encounters in this year of battles, of which the names are lost. Altogether, nine actions occurred, and nine Danish jarls and a king were killed. For the Danes, this state of perpetual warfare might be called their normal life, but for the Saxons the continued effort was too much. They were amateurs, members of a part-time army, and their resistance was subject to the law of diminishing returns. The civilian population was being worn down, and still their enemies did not leave them in peace.

This must have been clear to Alfred, and it is not surprising that he decided to come to terms with the Danes. The exact arrangement is uncertain: the *Chronicle* says simply "the West Saxons made peace with the Great Army"; Asser writes "the Saxons made a treaty with the heathen, on condition that they left the country." It was four months before the Danes moved out of Wessex—and, when they did at last go, no doubt they were well paid to do so.

Wessex had paid Danegeld for the first time. Was this, then, a humiliating surrender? Much depends on what the Danes had hoped to achieve when they entered the kingdom nine months earlier and fortified that base at Reading. If their object was simply to live off the countryside, to raid and to plunder, then they had not done too badly and they might consider it a year well-spent. If, on the other hand, they were looking for land, their hopes had been frustrated. Wessex had not gone the way of Northumbria and East Anglia. Alfred and the West Saxons had bought a breathing-space. Morale had been strengthened, for Alfred had kept his people's faces to the enemy. He had held the invader off, and then bought a tolerable peace. This was the behaviour of a statesman.

Alfred's resistance paid dividends. For the best part of five years the Danes left Wessex in peace. In 871 they wintered in London. Halfdan, the Danish leader, must have had some sort of settled government there, for coins were minted in the city at his command.

In the summer of 872 the Great Army moved north again to Northumbria. Egbert, the puppet ruler they had installed there (the Danes, like a later conqueror, chose when possible to hold their gains by quislings), had been overthrown by a popular uprising and had fled, together with the archbishop of York, to Mercia. The Danes did what they could to repair the situation in the north, and then wintered at Torksey, ten miles or so to the east of Lincoln. From there they could keep an eye on both their conquests, Northumbria and East Anglia.

The summer of the following year was spent in plundering the rich farmlands of the Lincoln area. Then in the autumn the Danes moved west into Mercia and took up their winter quarters at Repton, one of the burial places of the kings of Mercia.

Perhaps Burhred, the king of Mercia, read the writing on the wall and understood its message for him. For the last two years the Danes had been ravishing his eastern lands, from London to the Peak. Now they were moving towards the centre of his kingdom. Unlike Alfred, Burhred made no attempt to fight back. Early in 874, he suddenly left Mercia, the land he had ruled for twenty-two years, and went to Rome. He settled there, died there, and was buried in St. Mary's Church in the Saxon quarter of the city, a lonely exile from the soggy Midlands. It was not uncommon, as we have seen, for Saxon kings to make a pilgrimage to Rome, but Burhred's flight in the face of the enemy can only have been actuated by despair.

Alfred's sister Ethelswith was the king of Mercia's wife. She stayed behind and presumably took refuge at Alfred's court. She remains a shadowy figure. Our only contact with her today is a heavy gold ring in the British Museum. On its face is an *Agnus Dei* in niello and, scratched inside the ring, the inscription— *Eathelswith Regina*. It was found in the nineteenth century at Aberford in Yorkshire, a long way from Mercia. Was it looted by the Danes and then lost from some baggage-roll?

Ethelswith seems to have remained at Alfred's court for about fourteen years. Then, when her brother had repelled the Danes and the land was enjoying a few years of peace, she left for Rome. Alfred was sending an embassy that year and, in view of the difficulties and dangers of the journey, it seems very likely that his sister used the official company as an escort. But she never reached Rome. She fell ill in north Italy, died, and was buried at Pavia in the plain of Lombardy, four hundred miles from her husband's grave in Rome.

After the flight of Burhred Mercian resistance collapsed and the country came under the control of the enemy. The Danes set up another puppet ruler, who promised to rule as their vassal. Of this disastrous betrayal the *Anglo-Saxon Chronicle* has this to say:

> The Great Army subdued the whole land of Mercia . . . and they gave the kingdom into the keeping of Ceolwulf, *a foolish king's thegn*; and he swore oaths to them and gave hostages that Mercia should be ready for them on whatever day they would have it and that he would be ready, himself and all who would follow him, for the use of the Danes.

These were terms of unconditional surrender. We know from other sources that Ceolwulf was also committed to raising a large tribute. Not surprisingly he has had a bad press, "an Englishman by race, but a barbarian in wickedness", "a half-man", "An Infamous *Renegado* of the *Saxons*"—this last from Sir John Spelman.

The unexpected collapse of Mercia, the largest Saxon kingdom, must have dismayed Alfred. Now Wessex was the only independent state left. The fall of Mercia, in its smaller way, can be compared with the fall of France in 1940. In each case the disaster was sudden and unforeseen; in each case there was a previous history of old rivalry and more recent alliance; in each case a whole flank of the land still unconquered was suddenly exposed to the enemy.

The fall of Mercia occurred in 874, but the final onslaught of the Danes on Wessex did not take place till 876. Meanwhile in the autumn of 874 the Danish army split into two parts, never to reunite. One part, under the victorious Halfdan, moved back into Northumbria where, since the recent rebellion, there were still dangerous mutterings against the invaders.

Once back in the north Halfdan spent a year wasting the land beyond the Tees and campaigning against the British of Strathclyde in the area of the Lake District. Perhaps these parts had been dabbling in Northumbrian politics, or perhaps the wily Viking leader was only "pacifying" his north-west frontier, preparatory to settling in the southern section of the kingdom.

Whatever the Danish motives for this harrying of the north, it successfully extinguished the last vestiges of peaceful civilization in the area. The monks of Lindisfarne who had survived the earlier destruction of Northumbrian independence, were now so terrified that they decided the time had come to move the body of St. Cuthbert from their monastery. On his deathbed the saint had declared

> . . . if necessity compel you to choose one of two evils, I would far rather that you take my bones out from their grave and depart hence . . . than that for any cause you should consent to iniquity and bow your necks to the yoke of unbelievers.

Now was the time. Into St. Cuthbert's coffin, ornamented with runes and Celtic patterns, were tumbled the bones of St. Aidan, the head of St. Oswald, St. Cuthbert's portable altar, and the Lindisfarne Gospels. For seven years the monks wandered "like sheep before wolves", carrying with them these assorted treasures. Many years later, when peace had come at last, they settled at Chester-le-Street, north of the Tyne. St. Cuthbert's body was the foundation on which the prestige of the great prince-bishopric of Durham was later raised. The manuscript of St. John's Gospel, found in the coffin of St. Cuthbert in 1104, is now at Stonyhurst, still in its seventh-century binding.

After harrying the north, Halfdan settled his men to the south of the Tyne in the area that later became Yorkshire. This, the first of three partitions of eastern England by the invaders, had a twofold significance. On the one hand, the Danes were clearly there to stay. When the *Chronicle* states that "Halfdan divided the Northumbrians' lands, and from then on his men ploughed and tilled them", it is recording as significant and shattering an event as that of the fateful winter, a quarter of a century earlier, when the Vikings first wintered in England. But there was another side to the settlement of Yorkshire. The pirates would become farmers. They would defend their homesteads, but they would no longer be a rootless, predatory, fighting force. The Yorkshire settlement is in fact the beginning of the Danelaw, of the creation of a Danish pattern of life that was to leave a permanent imprint on the area. With this settlement Halfdan passes out of recorded history. In later centuries chroniclers, always anxious to score a theological point, claimed that God's vengeance on the heathen leader took the form of madness and an unbearable stench, so that even his own followers avoided him.

While one half of the Great Army was settling in the north, the remainder was on the move once more. Under three new leaders —Amund, Oskytel, and Guthrum—it left Repton and moved into East Anglia, setting up its winter quarters at Cambridge, where it remained for a year.

At this point in the surviving records, King Alfred appears on the scene again, for the first time since his treaty with the Danes in the autumn of 871. Alfred's life is full of gaps, and this is one of the most frustrating. One would give much to know how Alfred, twenty-two years old but already the veteran of half a dozen engagements, set about ruling the kingdom that had come, a little unexpectedly, to him. An interpolation in Asser states that "at the beginning of his reign, when he was a youth, and influenced by youthful emotions, he would not listen to the petitions which his subjects made to him for help in their difficulties, or for relief from those who oppressed them; but he repulsed them, and paid no attention to their requests." Unfortunately, this is a later monastic entry designed to show Alfred's tribulations at the hands of the Danes as the reproof of God. When he has accepted the reproof, the tide turns, and he is victorious. "Unfortunately", because a period of youthful tyranny would add light and shade to his life, just as Prince Hal's wild youth adds another dimension to

Henry V's character. But in fact there is no real evidence for the monastic fiction.

In a preface to his will Alfred himself describes how his title was confirmed by the witan:

> "I brought the will of King Ethelred to our meeting at Long Dean, and it was read aloud to the councillors. When it had been read I prayed them all, by the love they bore me, not to hesitate to declare the law, and I promised that I would never bear them a grudge, lest any man should say I wronged my kin. . . . Then they all judged, and said that they could not think of a more just right than mine. . . ."

Some shipbuilding took place during these lost years apparently. For in the summer of 875, when Halfdan was in Northumbria and Guthrum was in East Anglia, other Vikings came against Alfred. These were perhaps free-lance raiders from France, or from the Irish seas. At all events, there is evidence that Alfred was out with a small fleet in the summer of 875, and a brief reference to an encounter in the Channel in which Alfred fought against six or seven shiploads of Vikings, taking one of the ships and putting the others to flight. In the next century his kinsman, Ethelweard writes:

> . . . in the summer Alfred put to sea with his naval force, and the pagan fleet met him, with seven tall ships; a battle ensues, the Danes are put to flight, and one of their ships is captured by the king.

But this was small beer compared with the dramatic events of 876–8, one of the most critical periods in Alfred's reign.

For suddenly, in the autumn of 876, the Great Army left Cambridge, where it had remained immobile for almost a year and, in one of those lightning rides across country of which the Vikings were past masters, swept through Wessex to take up new quarters on the Dorset coast. The spot chosen was the Saxon town of Wareham and it was the usual excellent choice as a base. The town was protected on three sides by water. To the north and south ran the Rivers Frome and Trent; to the east was Poole Harbour—an important point this, since the Danes had arranged that a sea-host should co-operate with the land-host. Soon there were

lying in Poole Harbour not only Viking long-ships from East
Anglia but also ones "from the west"—from Ireland or from
Viking groups in South Wales.

Wessex was in danger of encirclement by sea and land.

The Danish base at Wareham was further protected by walls
and ditches—the green banks of the Saxon wall can still be
climbed today, a thousand years afterwards, a unique experience.
Within those walls the Danes lay secure and dangerously close to
Wimborne, Dorchester and Sherborne.

Nevertheless, the potential danger from the Danish occupation
of Wareham remained unfulfilled, for although Alfred was taken
by surprise, he raised the fyrd quickly and seems to have been
able to contain, if not to dislodge, his enemies. He probably
occupied the neck of land to the west between the two rivers and
then showed himself ready to fight or to pay the Danes to go
away. Once again peace was made. Once again the Danes swore to
leave Wessex. They gave hostages. They took their most solemn
oath, swearing by their great gold armlets—which they sprinkled
with blood and laid on an altar—an oath that Odin himself had
once taken and which, it was said, "they would never before do
for any people".

Then they broke their word.

The Saxons seem to have relaxed their control over the land
route out of Wareham and the Danes made a dash for it. "Acting
falsely, according to their usual custom," says Asser bitterly, "and
regarding neither their oath, nor the hostages, nor their promise,
they broke the treaty one night," and although Alfred rode hard
with the mounted men of the fyrd, he could not overtake them
before they reached the security of Exeter, seventy miles to the
west.

On the front at Swanage, sandwiched between the pin-tables
and the ice-cream stalls, there is a granite pillar about twenty feet
high, surmounted by four cannon-balls:

In commemoration of a great naval battle fought with the Danes in
Swanage Bay by Alfred the Great, A.D. 877.
Erected by John Mowlem, A.D. 1862.

Those inappropriate cannon-balls celebrate in fact an occasion on
which luck was on Alfred's side. The Danish fleet had moved out

of the shelter of Poole harbour with the intention of moving west to join the army at Exeter when it was caught off Swanage by an unexpected storm. The *Chronicle* says that one hundred and twenty ships were lost. If the figure is even approximately correct, this could mean the loss of anything up to five thousand men. As with the Spanish Armada seven hundred years later—*Deus afflavit et dissipati sunt*, "God blew and they were scattered". The combined operation against Wessex was at an end. This, the Saxons must have felt, was the natural reward for oath-breaking!

The Danes spent about eight months at their new base. Exeter was another typical Danish choice, protected by water, a walled town with an anchorage outside; from their point of view an ideal place in which to winter. But, as at Wareham, Alfred seems to have kept the enemy pretty well contained. Perhaps the Danes had hoped that the Celts in Cornwall would revolt as they had done once before in Egbert's time. If so, they were disappointed, and in the autumn they again made peace. This time they kept their word, leaving Wessex and moving north into Mercia where they set up their headquarters for the winter at Gloucester.

Now these Danes apparently followed the example of their northern compatriots. The *Chronicle* says that they divided Mercia "and shared out part of it" and the rest they gave to Ceolwulf the "unwise thegn" who was their puppet ruler in Mercia. Historians disagree as to what land the Danes occupied. It seems reasonable to assume that when Alfred later left the Danes in possession of a part of Mercia, that part was the area they had already settled. Mercia was now divided diagonally along a line running south-east from modern Liverpool to London, following the Roman road of Watling Street, the present-day A5. To the east of this line the Danes probably settled in the area that soon became known as that of "the Five Boroughs"—the land of which Lincoln, Nottingham, Derby, Leicester and Stamford formed regional Danish centres.

Whether or not this identification of the area of Danish settlement is correct, one thing is clear. Guthrum's army took no part in it. While his two companions fade out of history into silence Guthrum remains firmly established at Gloucester, poised on the frontier of Wessex. And after five months the Danish leader struck south again. In doing so he rang up the curtain on the mos critical and dramatic period in the long struggle between Alfred and the Danes.

Three times in seven years the enemy struck at Wessex: in 871 from their base at Reading; in 876 and 877 from southern bases at Wareham and Exeter; now, finally, from the north, from Gloucester. This time the affair was to be fought to a conclusion.

The Year of Decision (878)

*Minds shall be harder, hearts keener, spirit the stronger,
as our might lessens. . . .*
                                  The Battle of Maldon, 991

WE do not know where King Alfred spent Christmas 877. This is unfortunate for, in the light of what was to follow, Alfred's whereabouts at that time assume considerable importance. Dorchester seems the most probable place. It lay conveniently near Exeter, where the king had been negotiating with the Danes a few months earlier; it was also the usual place for the West Saxon court to spend Christmas.

Let us assume then, that Alfred was in Dorset, celebrating the Twelve Days of Christmas and enjoying a period of recreation after the long siege of Exeter. The fyrd would have disbanded and the Saxon thegns gone home with their men; having been kept under arms during so much of the year, they would be experiencing the usual war-weariness. Only the king's bodyguard would be with him.

This was the moment at which Guthrum and the Danes chose to invade Wessex once more.

Shortly after Twelfth Night 878, Guthrum broke camp and moved swiftly and silently into Alfred's kingdom. He seized the royal manor of Chippenham, 35 miles to the south. From this base the army was able to dominate all Wessex to the east of Somerset and Devon. "They overran," says the *Chronicle*, "the land of the West-Saxons and occupied it, and drove over sea many of the people, and they conquered most of the rest, and forced them to submit." Asser, hearing the story from Alfred, uses almost the same words: "There they wintered, and drove many of the people of Wessex overseas by force of arms, and through lack of the necessities of life. They reduced to almost complete subjection all the people of the country."

Other sources confirm this picture of the all but total collapse of Wessex. There are French records of fugitives from England, and a Saxon charter has survived recording the later confiscation of an ealdorman's lands for the crime of deserting Alfred at this time. The fugitives seem to have been mainly men of Hampshire. Having just, as they thought, seen the enemy leave Wessex for the time being, one can imagine the consternation of the local thegns when Danish bands suddenly appeared out of the blue, in the depths of winter, riding down the Roman road to Winchester.

This central part of Wessex, the area covered by Wiltshire and Hampshire, was now thoroughly pillaged for the first time. Alfred, in one of his translations written years afterwards, recalls "before it had all been ravaged and burnt, the churches all over England were full of treasures and books". Was this a first-hand memory of the pillaging of Wessex, or only a second-hand description of the general effect of the Viking raids?

Why did Wessex, which had resisted so many Danish attacks with some success, collapse so easily on this occasion? Guthrum's march on Chippenham clearly caught Alfred unawares. Not because, as is sometimes suggested, it took place in midwinter. The Danes had broken camp at that season before. Alfred's first great victory, at Ashdown, had been won on 8th January. But on that occasion the Saxon army, the fyrd, was under arms. This time they had just gone home, since the land was at peace, weary with a season's campaigning. The surprise lay not in the time of year, but in an attack coming so soon after the Danish evacuation of the kingdom. After Ashdown they had left Wessex alone for almost five years; after the retreat from Exeter they did not leave it alone for even five months.

Alfred had only his royal bodyguard immediately available as a fighting force. The Danish army, on the other hand, was always under arms. Guthrum had at last caught Alfred unprepared.

The consequence of Guthrum's strategy was thus the collapse of resistance in Wessex. He must have been very well satisfied with the results of his *coup* as, feasting at Chippenham, he watched his raiding parties returning laden with booty. But what was Guthrum's further aim? Was it merely to continue raiding the rich farmlands of central Wessex, or was it to conquer, to reduce to dependence, and finally to settle, the last of the independent

Saxon kingdoms, as other leaders in their turn had reduced and settled Northumbria, East Anglia and half of Mercia? On the answer to this question turns to some extent one's estimate of the importance of Alfred's reaction to the Danish success.

It is generally considered probable that Guthrum's plan in 878 was a revised edition of his scheme in 877. In that year, it will be remembered, he had been in touch with Viking fleets "from the west". Now there seems to have been renewed contact with one of the sons of Ragnar, who was wintering in South Wales, and a plan for a landing by his forces in Devonshire. That might lead to a rising of the Cornish. A pincer movement from Devon and from Chippenham would crack the resistance of Wessex. Finally, when Alfred was destroyed, the last Saxon kingdom would have been eliminated and Guthrum's army might have land for the asking.

If Guthrum's plan, as outlined above, was one of conquest, then the success or failure of Alfred's resistance becomes immeasurably more significant than if the king were only engaged in pushing back Danish raiders.

It is now time to consider Alfred's movements. When the *Chronicle* recorded "they conquered most of the rest and forced them to submit", it added the significant words *"except King Alfred*, and he with a small band of followers went with difficulty to the woods and the fastnesses of the moors".

These were the woods and flooded plains of Somerset. When Alfred pondered on the probable schemes of Guthrum, he could see that if resistance was to be carried on it must be a resistance based on Western Somerset and Devon. The open country of Wiltshire and Hampshire was indefensible, but the west was protected from the enemy by physical obstacles. A belt of thickly wooded country, the forest of Selwood, ran south from the River Avon near Chippenham to the borders of Dorset. Behind those wooded heights lay the Somerset Levels, fen country like that of East Anglia. At the best of times this was a poor land of alder thicket and peat bog, and in the early part of the year, when the spring tides were backed up by gales from the west, a large part of it was flooded to a depth of five or six feet. Even today, with all the resources of modern drainage, this land is liable to flood for some time in the winter.

From behind these obstacles Alfred might hope to deliver, with the help of his bodyguard of king's thegns, guerrilla attacks against Guthrum's forces.

Moreover, by retreating to the west, the king lay between the Danish army and the possible invasion from South Wales. Alfred must be where he could move east or west with equal facility. It was the position of maximum danger—but considerations of that sort never seem to have had much weight with the king.

Asser confines his account to the bare facts:

> At the same time Alfred . . . with a few of his nobles, and some soldiers and vassals, passed a restless time in much anxiety among the woods and marshy tracts of Somerset. They had none of the necessities of life, except what they took, either openly or craftily, by frequent assaults, from the Danes and from those Christians who had submitted to the Danish rule.

The king and his freedom fighters, then, carried on a successful guerrilla warfare from the West Country "jungle". But this was not the way to defeat the Danes. For that an army would be needed. When the Danes seized Chippenham, there was no Saxon force in existence, yet four months later Alfred was able to lead a regular army against the enemy and beat them. To understand how the king was able to achieve this remarkable reversal of fortune it is necessary to know something of the structure of the Saxon army at this time.

There were four types of fighting man at the disposal of a Saxon king. First and foremost was the king's bodyguard, the king's thegns at court. Some were men who held high rank, others were mere followers, the king's retainers maintained by food-rents. This bodyguard probably numbered two or three hundred. When Alfred's forerunner, Cynewulf, king of Wessex, was caught and killed, eighty-four men—his bodyguard—were slain with him. Alfred's bodyguard in time of war would certainly be larger than this. These were the men who were with him at court when the Danes struck and who followed him into Somerset.

Just as the king had his bodyguard, so each ealdorman had his followers and retainers, his personal "hearthband", and he could also call on the support of the thegns of his shire, who were under an obligation to fight to the death for their ealdorman. Ethelnoth, ealdorman of Somerset, with his body guard, had joined Alfred's little band.

Thirdly there were the remaining thegns of the shire—local farmers, each responsible for attending with their own followers. The horsemen were armed with helmet and mail shirt (byrnie), sword, spear and shield. The footmen might have byrnies and axes, or flails and cudgels.

The fourth group was composed of the ordinary freemen, or ceorls. They worked with the army, carrying food, digging fortifications, and in some cases fighting.

Apart from the king's retainers, and the ealdorman's hearth-band, the Saxon army was very much a body of amateurs. It took some time to assemble. It was composed of peasants and farmers who had other jobs to do and who could not leave their fields for long, particularly at the critical seasons of spring and late summer, and who would not fight for many weeks in districts far from their wives and families. If kept in the field for long periods of time, the fyrd was always liable to melt away. Two centuries later, Harold's defeat by William the Conqueror was largely due to the fact that the Saxon army had been kept in a state of readiness all through the summer, waiting for a threatened invasion that never materialized, and had then been allowed to return to its local districts in the autumn.

When Alfred had helped to win the battle of Ashdown, the fyrd had been in the field, and fresh. Now the fyrd was not mobilized. It would take time to call together, and it could not, in any case, be summoned immediately. For there were two periods in the Saxon year when the men—or some of them at least—must be working on the land or famine and starvation would follow. One of these periods was in the late summer and early autumn when all hands were needed for the harvest and the autumn sowing. The second was the time of the spring sowing, calculated as lasting from Candlemas (2nd February) to Easter.

In 878 Easter fell on 23rd March. During the months of February and March, therefore, it would be unwise—and probably impossible—to gather the fyrd together. After that it would take some weeks for the local levies to assemble. Somehow Alfred must keep the flame of resistance burning without the support of the main Saxon army until May, a period of seventeen or eighteen weeks after the Danish swoop on Chippenham. Somehow that period must be bridged.

Hence the retreat to Somerset, the days when Alfred with his little band "went with difficulty to the woods and fastnesses of the moors". Hence, too, the continual harassing of the Danes "by frequent assaults". Time must be won for the spring sowing, and for the shire levies to assemble after that.

Time was the essence of the matter.

There was, it is true, an alternative course of action. Alfred could leave the country as his brother-in-law King Burhred of Mercia had recently done and as his own men of Hampshire were now doing. . . . It was not, apparently, an alternative that found favour in Alfred's eyes.

Was it really possible to drive the Danes out of Wessex, now that they had got this flying start? The enemy had many advantages. They had better weapons—the long-sword with tapering sides and the two-handed axe—and better discipline. Their battle tactics were sound, their ferocious reputation unnerving. They had no fields that needed attention, no homesteads to protect: they were a professional army living off somebody else's lands. Yet there were certain encouraging signs of weakness. The Danish army was not getting any larger. There had been no recent reinforcements from overseas, and those who had fought so long in England were showing signs of wanting to settle down. Defeat might bring disagreement. But could the Vikings be defeated?

To Alfred, weighing the pros and cons with anxious care, it seemed that they could. The Danes had triumphed in the past through the weaknesses of their enemies. The Irish and Northumbrians had gone under because they had been hopelessly disunited. The East Anglians had trafficked with the invader. The King of Mercia had run away. It was time that somebody stood up and fought back.

Moreover the men of Wessex had won great victories under Alfred's grandfather Egbert, and under his father Ethelwulf. Within the last ten years they had sent one army packing from before Winchester, and he himself had played a large part in the defeat of the Great Army at Ashdown. Wessex was strong in unity and patriotism. The fyrd was well-knit in local units each under its own ealdorman. What they had done before they could do again . . . given time.

And what about the Danes in South Wales? If Alfred knew of Guthrum's plans for a joint invasion—and it would appear that he was expecting trouble from the west—their possible arrival must have seemed the one incalculable factor in the military equation. Supposing they landed when the Saxon army was fully engaged with the main Danish armies farther east? That was a question which admitted of no clear answer.

Suddenly the situation became clearer.

Some time before Easter there came the feared attack from the west. A fleet of twenty-three ships put out from Pembrokeshire and crossed to the north Devon coast. It was led by one of Ragnar Leather-breeches' sons, traditionally supposed, on rather slender evidence, to have been called Ubbe.

The men of Devon, under their ealdorman Odda, retreated before the enemy to Cynuit, the strongpoint of Countisbury Hill, on the coast halfway between Minehead and Ilfracombe. Cynuit was a well-defended hillfort, commanding the coast road to the east. To realize just how well-defended it was one should go and stand today on the cliffs there and see the land fall away on three sides, a thousand feet in a quarter of a mile.

This was a decisive moment for Wessex and, fortunately, Asser describes in some detail what followed:

> When the Danes saw that the fortress was altogether unprepared and unfortified, they began to lay siege to it. They did not try to storm it because the place was impregnable and secure on all sides except on the eastern (as we have ourselves seen). In besieging it they thought that those who were inside would soon surrender from hunger and thirst, since the fortress had no water-supply.
>
> But things did not fall out as they had expected. For the defenders attacked the heathen suddenly at dawn, and at the first onslaught they cut down the Danes in great numbers, including their king. Only a few escaped by flight to their ships.
>
> There the Saxons took much spoil. And amongst other things the banner which men call "the Raven". They say that the three sisters of Ingvar and Ubbe, the daughters of Ragnar Leather-breeches, wove that banner in a single day. They say moreover that, in every battle in which the banner went before the Danes, the raven in the middle of the design seemed to flutter as though it were alive, if they

were going to win. But if the Danes were going to lose the battle, it would hang down motionless. And this was often proved to be true.

(Sir John Spelman comments sardonically on the magic standard: "Whatsoever it was, the Imposture was now betrayed: for being taken by surprise, they had lost their Oracle before they had time to consult with it.")

The Saxon success at Countisbury can be seen as the turning point in the campaign. Relieved of the threat from the west, Alfred was able to adopt a more aggressive attitude towards the Danes to the east. His resistance enters what may be called "phase two". The king moved after Easter to Athelney with his guerrilla fighters, and built a fort there. "And from this fort," says Asser, "he made frequent assaults upon the heathen."

The island of Athelney was a little patch of ground, less than thirty acres in area, rising about forty feet above the surrounding thickets and swamps. Visit Athelney today in summer, and there is nothing remarkable about the site. To the west of Athelney "Hill" runs the main road to Glastonbury, from which a country road forks to disappear to the east. The rise is so slight as to be unremarkable if it were not for a small monument, a truncated obelisk put up in 1801, on the skyline. There is nothing else to be seen, no ruins, no "remains". The things that catch the eye are the bundles of withies—stripped willow shoots—lying in golden rows against the railings. But go there in a bad winter, when the floods are up and the roads three foot deep in water, and the low rise is once more an island, impressive in its bleak isolation.

There were other islands in the Somerset Levels, but Athelney was peculiarly suited to Alfred's purposes. Although surrounded by marsh, it lay very close to the higher ground. Only a mile or two to the south was the village of Lyng, where there were royal estates and a dry route to the west country. Half a dozen miles to the east was the road leading to the Danish-controlled—or at any rate Danish-raided—area of Wessex.

In later centuries it was around this island of Athelney, the one identifiable spot connected with Alfred's activities as a guerrilla fighter, that the legends clustered and multiplied.

It was from Athelney, men said, that Alfred had gone, with one faithful companion, disguised as a wandering minstrel, to the

Danish camp, "and by the Privilege of that Disguise, had free Admittance everywhere even into the King's Tents," says Spelman, and learnt the Danish plans.

It was at Athelney, people claimed, that Alfred burnt the cakes. A subsequent addition to Asser's *Life* describes how Alfred was living *incognito* in a cowherd's hut. The cowherd's wife "being busied one day in going to the Oven with Bread, and having set a Cake thereof before the fire (where the King sat trimming of his Bow and arrows, and fitting his other Weapons), while she went about her Business, the Cake burnt, and the King, wholly intent to the fitting of his Tackle, minded it not, 'till the rude Huswife coming in, and finding the Cake burning, in a great Chase fell on scolding at the King.

> Canst sit and see the Bread burn thus, thou sot,
> And canst not turn what thou so well lov'st hot?"

That was how they told the tale in the seventeenth century.

From Athelney, and perhaps also from another patch of higher ground a mile to the north, Alfred and his men harried the Danes, while the county levies assembled secretly—for Alfred had gained the time he needed, and now the spring sowing was over. Then, in the seventh week after Easter (4th–11th, May), the King struck.

At the southern end of Selwood Forest stood "Egbert's Stone" marking the point where the limits of Wiltshire, Somerset and Dorset met. That point is traditionally said to be the site of the eighteenth-century "King Alfred's Tower", two or three miles to the north of the junction of the modern county boundaries and lying about twenty-five miles due east of Athelney on the crest of the hills. This was the secret meeting-place, and all day men gathered there from Somerset, Wiltshire and the west of Hampshire.

There Alfred met them:

And when they saw the king they received him like one risen from the dead, after so great tribulation, and they were filled with great joy.

So Asser, remembering no doubt that it was Ascension-tide.

The *Anglo-Saxon Chronicle* records more simply, "and they were fain of him"—that is to say, "they were glad to see him."

Speed was now most important. Alfred and his army lay for one night at Egbert's Stone and then on the following morning they broke camp and marched north-east to *Iglea*. This was probably the spot now known as Eastleigh Wood, two miles to the south of Warminster, where there was once an *Iley* Oak, a day's march of about eleven miles. There they spent the second night.

At dawn the army was on the move again. That day they met the Danish army at *Ethandun*.

As usual, the exact site of the battle is uncertain. "Ethandun" is the modern village of Edington, lying at the foot of Salisbury Plain on the north side and about a dozen miles south of the Danish base at Chippenham. To reach Edington from Alfred's night camp at Iglea, the army would first have to march up on to the north-west corner of Salisbury Plain. In one of his translations Alfred writes as though he thought that battles were always fought on "downs", and it is reasonable to assume that Ethandun was fought somewhere on Salisbury Plain itself, to the south of the village of Edington.

At this point the Plain is about 5 miles wide, and as to the exact spot between its northern and southern edges—well, each historian can back his fancy. The ground is seamed with ditches and earthworks, the scribble and scars of forgotten encounters. There are two probable sites. One is on the southern edge, about three miles north-east of Eastleigh. Here the slope is guarded by a ditch and would have provided a good defensive position for the Danes, overlooking as it did the Saxon line of approach, if they could get there in time.

The other possible site is 3 miles farther on, at the northern edge of the Plain, and commanding the Danish route from Chippenham. Here, at Bratton Castle, there is a Bronze Age fort and another White Horse, said to have been cut by Alfred's command. The horse in its present form was in fact cut in 1778, but it overlies a smaller horse, facing in the opposite direction, and it is no longer possible, of course, to date this earlier figure, though modern opinion suspects that it is not much older than the present horse.

As between these two sites there is little to choose in the shape of evidence. One must pay one's money and take one's pick: the balance of opinion inclines to the northern site above Bratton Castle. What is quite certain, however, is that one of the decisive battles in European history took place somewhere on this bare, pinched-off corner of Salisbury Plain.

Some time in the early morning—Alfred, it will be remembered, had left Eastleigh at dawn, about five-thirty at this time of year—the two armies faced one another. The lengthy preliminaries essential to any battle at this time would have been the same as those at the earlier battle of Ashdown. The careful marshalling of one's men (there were probably three or four thousand on each side at Ethandun), the shouts and clashing of arms to terrify the enemy, the inspection of the shield-wall by the leaders —these were standard practice. The formality of the opening moves makes a piquant contrast with the unplanned hand-to-hand struggles between little knots of men into which a battle usually developed fairly quickly.

So much we can assume of the fighting at Ethandun. It would be satisfying to have a full description of this, Alfred's greatest battle, but the details available are disappointingly meagre: the Chronicle states simply that Alfred "there fought against the whole of the Great Army and put them to flight and rode after them as far as their camp". Asser adds the information that Alfred formed his men into a close shield-wall—shield locked with shield—and that after he had pursued the Danes to their stronghold, he seized everything outside, men and horses and cattle. "The men he killed, the beasts he carried off, and then he pitched camp boldly with all his men before the camp."

For the scene at Ethandun one must use one's imagination therefore, fuelled by contemporary accounts of other battles. The description in the Old English poem *Judith* fits the general pattern of Ethandun reasonably accurately:

> The valiant men and warriors marched out, bore banners of victory; they set straight forward to the fight . . . at break of dawn; the shield rang, resounded loudly. The lean wolf in the wood rejoiced at that, and the dark raven, the bird greedy for slaughter; both knew that the warriors purposed to provide them with a feast of fated men; and behind them flew the dewy-feathered eagle, hungry for food; dark-coated, horny-beaked, it sang a song of war. The men of

battle marched on, warriors to the strife, protected by shields, hollow linden targes,—they who once had borne the flaunting of foreigners, the taunt of the heathen. . . . Then keenly they shot forth showers of arrows, adders of war, from their bows of horn, strong shafts; the raging warriors loudly stormed, cast spears into the press of brave men; wroth were the heroes, the dwellers in the land, against the hateful race; sternly they stepped forward; stout of heart, they harshly aroused their ancient foes. . . . The men with their hands drew from the sheaths the brightly adorned blades with trusty edges; fiercely they smote . . . they spared no living man of the host, mean or mighty, whom they could overcome. So all morning the noble warriors pursued the foreign people.

After the battle Alfred pursued the Danes to their camp, which is generally assumed to have been their base at Chippenham, a dozen miles to the north of Ethandun. There he besieged the Danes for a fortnight. At the end of that time the enemy capitulated—suddenly and completely. The Danes sued for terms to the man who a short month earlier had been an apparently throneless king. It is this startling reversal of fortune that has caught the imagination of men ever since. As has been seen, there are grounds for believing that Alfred at Athelney was not so powerless a figure as has often been assumed. At the same time, though he knew that the Saxon fyrd was gathering, there was nothing that could lead him to assume the decisive victory of Ethandun and the surrender of the enemy a fortnight later.

Asser gives as the reasons for that surrender "hunger and cold, fear and despair". The "cold" seems improbable, even in an English May, but Alfred's destruction of all supplies outside the camp may easily have played a decisive part in the sudden decision of the Danes. Perhaps, too, Guthrum was having trouble with his men. . . .

Whatever the reasons, the Danes accepted humiliating terms. They swore to leave Wessex, their king Guthrum was to be baptized, and Alfred was to take what hostages he would to ensure that these terms were carried out. "Never before," says Asser, "had they made peace with anyone on such terms."

The Danish army remained for the summer at Chippenham, and then left Wessex, wintering at Cirencester in the former kingdom of Mercia. But three weeks after the treaty of Chippenham, their leader Guthrum and thirty companions rode south to meet Alfred at the church at Aller, near Athelney. Six weeks earlier Alfred had been living, with a handful of followers, the uncertain life of a guerrilla leader in these swamps. Now he stood godfather to his defeated rival, heard Guthrum baptized with the Saxon name of Athelstan, "noble stone", and himself "raised him from the sacred font".

One must not make too much of the actual ceremony of Guthrum's baptism. There is a famous story of a Viking in continental Europe who boasted that he had been baptized twenty times already and went on to complain that the baptismal robe for the twenty-first ceremony was not up to standard. Nevertheless, the ceremony must have been something of a humiliation if Guthrum did not believe, while if he did then it must have been highly impressive.

After the baptism at Aller Alfred took Guthrum and his followers back to the royal palace at Wedmore, a few miles to the north-west on the slopes of the Mendips. There the Danes remained for twelve days as Alfred's guests. This is significant. Formerly the Vikings had reluctantly given promises, and then hurried away to break them. One can see in this relatively prolonged intercourse, the first sign of Alfred's policy that Saxon and Dane must learn to co-exist.

On the eighth day Guthrum's "chrism-loosing" took place. The ealdorman of Somerset, Ethelnoth, performed the ceremony. At baptism a linen cloth was bound in the form of a cross round the head, to protect the chrism, the holy oil. For a week afterwards the newly-baptized would wear white and then on the eighth day, the cloth was taken off and the robes laid aside. After that came the feasting and drinking and the mutual exchange of presents.

When Guthrum at last left Wedmore for Chippenham, Alfred must have watched with mingled feelings as the Danes rode off and disappeared from view over the crest of the Mendips. It had been a great victory, and Wessex was saved—for the moment. Guthrum and he had lived and talked together—there had been the magic of personality as well as the magic of religion. But the Danes had broken their word so many times. What was going to happen now?

Two things in fact happened. The first was that Alfred received news of another fleet of Danish ships, which had sailed up the Thames and encamped at Fulham. There was a strong rumour that they were in touch with Guthrum. (In fact, the two forces were not working together but Alfred did not know that.) It was a disturbing thought. However, after wintering in England, the newcomers left again the following November as mysteriously as they had come, making for the Low Countries. That was good.

The second event was even better. Guthrum and his force spent almost a year in western Mercia, disturbingly close to the borders of Wessex—and then they quietly moved away into East Anglia and settled there. "The Great Army fared from Cirencester into East Anglia and occupied the land and divided it out," says the *Chronicle*. It was the autumn of 879. Only then could Alfred know that his victory at Ethandun had been a real one.

The Reorganization of the Kingdom

These are a king's materials, and the tools with which he governs: a land well-peopled with men of prayer, men of war, and men of work. Without these tools no king can do his work.

King Alfred's translation of Boethius

FOUR times already during Alfred's reign the Danes had struck at Wessex. Once from the east in 871, using Reading as a base; twice from the south, in 876 and 877, from the ports of Wareham and Exeter; finally, in 878, from western Mercia by way of Chippenham. On the last three occasions they had had some support from Viking fleets operating in the Irish Sea area. Alfred had weathered these storms, but there was no guarantee that Wessex was out of danger. On the contrary, it was more than likely that the enemy would come again.

The immediate tasks were obvious. Wessex must be made strong in men, in ships, in forts. The Danish hold on western Mercia and on London must be tested. These were clear necessities. But the king took a more comprehensive view. Learning and law too must be restored and the arts of civilization recovered. The future relations between Dane and Saxon must be considered, the two races would have to learn to live with one another. Perhaps there might have to be some sort of division of the island if there was ever to be peace in the land.

All this Alfred attempted to achieve during the next twenty years. It is this broad view of the problems facing him, a view that could include fortifications and books, church services and treaties, which raises Alfred above the level of the successful soldier, and places him in the ranks of the statesmen. To defeat the Danes was one thing, to make Wessex both secure and civilized was quite another.

There was never very long when Alfred could give his undivided attention to the arts of peace, but there were periods of quiescence, periods when a far-sighted man might take advantage of a temporary lull in the Viking pressure to consider what could be done to strengthen and to refine his kingdom. During the fourteen years between 878 and 892 England was more often at peace than at war and it was during these years that Alfred carried out most of the constructive measures on which one aspect of his claim to greatness rests.

The question of defence must be given priority, for at any moment the Danes might strike again. Here the largest problem, in every sense of the word, was that of the protection of the frontiers against a surprise attack. Again and again the Danes had been able to seize a town and use it as a base before the Saxons were even aware that they were on the move. Wessex was peculiarly vulnerable to this strategy. At no point was it more than about 35 miles from either the long, exposed sea-coast or from the borders of Danish-occupied Mercia.

When they had seized a fortified town, or created one—their first action was always to throw up an earthwork—they were secure. The Saxons might defeat the Danes in the field, but they had suffered heavy losses whenever they had tried to storm a fortified position.

Alfred, who learnt quickly by experience, argued that if a Danish garrison could hold a town against all attacks, then so could a Saxon one. He therefore began to construct a great system of fortified strong-points round the borders of Wessex. The king may have got a hint also from the fortified towns of Charles the Great, and from those that the emperor's descendants had been lately constructing in neighbouring Flanders.

In England the thegns owed three duties to their kind—those of fighting for him, of bridge-building, and of *burhbot*, the construction of town fortifications. Alfred thus had ready to hand the administrative machinery with which to put into effect his strategic plan for a ring of fortified posts around the borders of his lands.

It was a long job. The work was not finished in Alfred's day, but the overall plan was his. The final picture emerges from a document known as the *Burghal Hidage*, compiled shortly after his death, about the years 911-19. From the list of fortified towns given there it is clear that Alfred, like all great men, worked with whatever material lay to hand. Here the existing walls of a Roman

town would be restored, as at Exeter; there the embankments of a
Saxon town such as Wareham would be extended and strengthened; a little isolated fort would become the nucleus of a burh,
as at Lydford in Devon; sometimes a brand-new burh would be
built, like the one at Athelney. Not all the work was done by the
king. An ealdorman or a churchman might have the duty—or
privilege—of constructing a new burh; Oxford and Wallingford
are probably examples of foundations of this type. In conception
the buhr was something more than a fort and less than a town, but
a site which was suited for defence was often suited for trade too,
and many of the burhs later developed into boroughs.

The *Burghal Hidage* contains the names of about thirty burhs
encircling Wessex. Kent is not in the list, probably because it
ranked as a sub-kingdom with its own organization, for there
were certainly the equivalent of the burhs of Wessex at such Kentish towns as Rochester, Canterbury and Dover.

The placing of the main burhs indicates the comprehensive
nature of Alfred's scheme quite clearly: in Sussex there were
coastal burhs at Hastings, Lewes, Chichester and Portchester.
Hampshire was covered by coastal defences at Southampton and
Christchurch. An inner line included Winchester, Wilton and
Shaftesbury. The western end of the Channel was guarded by
Wareham and Bridport in Dorset, and Exeter in Devon. At this
point the line turned north; Cornwall was not in the scheme. On
the north Devon coast there was a burh at Pilton, near Barnstaple.
Somerset was defended by Watchet on the coast and by the inland burhs of Athelney, Axbridge and Bath. Along the northern
frontier, which was bordered by friendly Mercia, the burhs were
fewer and the districts they dominated correspondingly larger.
Malmesbury, Cricklade, Oxford, Wallingford and Buckingham
brought the line back along the northern side of the Thames
valley to the last burh at Southwark. The scheme was all-embrac-
ing, and Alfred knew he would not live to see it completed. Asser
complained that some of the forts which Alfred had ordered to be
built were never begun "or, being begun late, were never finished"
before the Danes came again. He goes on to say that when it was
too late, "these saboteurs of the royal ordinances repented, and
blushed at their non-performance of the king's commands."

The *Chronicle* records an attack on a half-finished fort in 892 at the very beginning of Alfred's last war against the Danes—and at just about the time when Asser was writing his *Life* and setting down the caustic comment just quoted. After describing a Danish landing at the mouth of the River Lymne in East Kent the *Chronicle* continues, "they rowed their ships upstream as far as the forest, four miles from the sea, *and there they stormed a fort. Inside the fort were a few ceorls and it was only half-built.*" It sounds very much as if the invaders came on the Saxon ceorls (peasants) in the act of throwing up the embankment for a new burh and took over their half-finished work.

When there were Roman or Saxon walls there for the strengthening, the process of constructing a burh probably consisted of raising an earth wall faced with turf and protected by a forward ditch and palisade. It is possible that the grass-covered banks still to be seen at Wallingford and at Wareham owe their present appearance to this period.

So much for the physical construction of a burh. But a fort that could be immediately held against a surprise Danish attack would need a permanent garrison as well. The exact method by which this garrison was obtained is not certain. It is clear that the forts *had* a garrison—the burhware—of fighting townsmen; most probably the thegns of each shire were ordered to maintain houses and retainers in the burhs of that shire. These fighting burgesses were responsible for the defences and for stockpiling provisions against the day when the countrymen from round about should need to seek shelter within the walls. Each fort held a garrison the size of which was in proportion to the length of wall to be maintained. In time of danger one man would be sent from each hide (anything from 40 to 120 acres) of land allotted for the town's upkeep. By this means, it was estimated, every pole of wall could be defended by four men.

It is possible to check this rather complicated mathematical system. The length of the medieval wall at Winchester, one of the largest burhs, was 3,280 yards. The *Burghal Hidage* allotted 2,400 men to its defence. These would be sufficient to man 600 poles, or 3,300 yards. The coincidence of this theoretical length with the actual length of the wall is remarkable. Similarly, at Wallingford the embankments measure 3,030 yards, as compared with a theoretical length of 3,300. At Wareham the actual length is

2,180, against a theoretical length of 2,200 yards. It is clear that the size of these garrisons represent real and exact necessities and are not symbolic figures of the kind so often come across in early times.

It came to be the custom that all necessary repairs to the walls were to be carried out in the fortnight after the Rogation Days which would usually fall in May—a comparatively slack time for the farmer. In return for these duties "the men who kept the burh" were exempt from service away from home with the national army.

The co-ordination of a large strategical plan and a detailed machinery for putting that plan into effect is one of the hallmarks of Alfred's greatness. And the system worked. In Alfred's last great war against the Danes (892–6) one finds the men who kept the burh holding up the invader's progress until the king, his son, or the local ealdorman of the shire can come up with a detachment of the fyrd.

The burhs would protect the frontier against a surprise attack, but an efficient, mobile army was also needed. The ordinary shire-band, the fyrd, had always suffered from the fact that it was composed of peasants and farmers, who could not leave their fields for long periods of time "for the Souldier at that time was fain to be both Souldier, Artificer, and Husbandman too" as Spelman puts it. The problem was urgent for Alfred, remembering the testing days at Athelney, when he had to hang on as best he could until it was possible to assemble the fyrd.

Again and again one finds Alfred learning by experience (a trait that does not appear, for instance, in the commanders of the First World War). The king divided the fyrd into two parts. In future, when one part was called up the other part would remain in the village, getting on with the work and at the same time available to defend the women and children if a surprise raid struck the area. The arrangement was made easier to introduce by the fact that in many ways the production of food was still a communal, co-operative activity.

An attempt was also made to see that the county organization was kept up to date and that men did not just evade service by transferring their allegiance from one lord to another. In chapter 37 of Alfred's Laws the king lays down:

If a man wishes to go from one district and seek a lord in another district he must do it with the knowledge of the ealdorman whom he formerly followed in his shire.

This was a simple and efficient solution to a difficult problem and in his later wars it enabled Alfred to keep an army in the field almost continuously. But it was not entirely foolproof. In the campaign of 893 Alfred's son, Edward the Elder, had the Danish army bottled up to the north of Staines. But the Saxon fyrd, having eaten its supplies and served its appointed time, went off home before the relief force which was to take over had arrived. As a result the Danes were able to break out of the trap and escape across country to their base in Essex.

The Danes operated by water as well as by land. If they were to be held, and perhaps repelled, ships would be needed as well as secure forts and a reliable army. Wessex appears to have had a fleet before the days of Alfred. In his father's time the Kentish fleet had defeated a great force at Sandwich, capturing nine ships, and Alfred, as has been seen, had taken part in a skirmish with six or seven Danish raiders in 875.

In 881, to look ahead for a moment, there was a second clash in which four ships were put to flight, and by 885 Alfred was able to send what the *Chronicle* describes as "a ship-army" to the coast of Danish-occupied East Anglia, where they captured sixteen Viking ships and won a real victory. These isolated incidents suggest the development of a force capable of outsailing and out-fighting the enemy, and this is confirmed by the one firm statement of Alfred's activities in this matter.

Then King Alfred ordered long ships to be built to counter the Danish ships; they were twice as long as the Danish light ships. Some had sixty oars and some had even more. They were swifter, steadier, and higher than the others. They were shaped neither in the Frisian manner nor in the Danish, but as it seemed to him that they might be most useful.

"*But as it seemed to him that they might be most useful*"; once again one recognizes the Alfred touch—the ability to adapt and improve an existing institution or implement to meet a new situation. Apart from Alfred, only Charles the Great and the Arab rulers of Spain saw clearly that the most effective way to beat the Vikings was to fight them on their chosen element, the sea, and prevent them from ever setting foot on land.

The new fleet was not always successful but it formed the basis of the English fleet of over a hundred ships that supported Saxon power in the next century. Alfred is one of half a dozen founders of the English navy.

The combined success of these military reforms—the new ships, the wall of burhs, the divided fyrd—was demonstrated in practice by the remarkable success of Alfred in his second great war against the Danes at the close of the century and of his reign.

Alfred was not content to let it rest at that. "While, therefore, his Sword had scarce well enough cleared the way unto his Scepter", the king turned his attention to the problem of government. Security—a matter of tangible creations, the hard wood of ships' keels, the earth walls rising round the burhs, the deployment of heavy Saxon ceorls—was for a ninth-century king an easy problem to solve compared with the restoration of the intangible values of order and justice to a land that had been raided and fought over, sacked and ravaged, intermittently for a generation. As always, Alfred saw the practical side of the problem—it was necessary to make the existing laws clear, and then to ensure that they were enforced. Alfred was by the year 890 in a position to issue his own codifications of the existing laws, his own *Doombook*.

The aim of Alfred's code is essentially conservative, the endowment of religion, the restoration of law, and the enforcement of justice as it had existed before the monasteries were, in the king's own words, "all harried and burnt", and before law and order had broken down through large parts of England. In his translation of Boethius, Alfred later wrote:

> I wanted tools and materials to carry on the work which I was set to do, which was that I should virtuously steer and direct the authority committed unto me. . . .

In this respect, a clear, enforceable law was both the anchor and the rudder.

Alfred's code was partly based on the earlier codes of three separate kingdoms, Wessex, Kent, and Mercia. To build on the work of others fits in with what we already know of Alfred's methods, but it may strike the twentieth-century observer as a little unadventurous. To feel this is to misunderstand Alfred's attitude. The passion for legislation is modern. As recently as the middle of the nineteenth century Palmerston, when Prime Minister, was able to say: "Oh! There is really nothing to be done. We cannot go on adding to the Statute Book *ad infinitum*." To the Saxon, and to men for centuries afterwards, it was not the king's duty to frame new laws, but to make clear and respected those that already existed—to *declare* the law. A lawgiver was the interpreter of eternal truths to his generation.

In the light of this attitude, Alfred's cautious introduction to his own *Doombook* is understandable:

> Now I, king Alfred, have gathered together these laws and I have ordered that many of those which our ancestors obeyed should be written out—those which seemed good to me. But many—those which did not seem good—I have rejected by the advice of my councillors; and in other cases I have ordered changes to be made. I dared not be so bold as to set down many of my own in writing, for I did not know which of these would please those who came after me. But of those laws dating from the time of Ine or Offa or Ethelbert I gathered together here such as seemed to me best, and the others I rejected. Then I, Alfred, king of the West Saxons, showed all these to my councillors, and they then said that it pleased them all to observe them.

In Alfred's code there is an attempt not only to unify the different Saxon codes, but also to reconcile three contrasting attitudes: the Roman, which saw in law the voice of government; the German, the voice of tradition; and the Hebrew, the voice of God. This last was to Alfred, as a Christian, particularly important. Parts of the Mosaic law are repeated and the Golden Rule of Christianity is quoted in its negative form: "that which ye will that other men should not do to you, that do ye not to them."

"From this one Doom," wrote Alfred, "a man may understand how he should judge everyone justly; he needs no other doombook. Let him judge a man as he himself would wish to be judged, if the other man were in his place."

In many parts of Europe the king's power to legislate was atrophying at this time from lack of use. Alfred's example kept the tradition alive in England.

The basic problem of the age, in Wessex as elsewhere in Europe, was that of the preservation of order. The main emphasis in Alfred's code is on the sanctity of oaths and agreements. These must be kept at all costs, for they are the foundations on which all civilized society—and particularly feudal society—rests; "In the first place, we insist, as a matter of supreme importance, that every man shall keep carefully his oath and his pledge."

From the ceorl to the king, everyone owes faith to the man above him, the ceorl to his thegn, the king at the top of the social skyscraper to God. The oath of allegiance to an overlord was the peg which held together this feudal structure. It ran as follows:

> By the Lord, before whom these relics are holy, I will be loyal and true to   —   —   , and love all that he loves, and hate all that he hates, in accordance with God's rights and secular obligations; and never, willingly and intentionally, in word or deed, do anything that is hateful to him; on condition that he keep me as I shall deserve, and carry out all that was our agreement, when I subjected myself to him and chose his favour.

It followed from this that the authority of superiors must be upheld, for ". . . Christ commanded that a lord should be loved as oneself . . .," said Alfred's code, and a later Saxon code declared even more explicitly, ". . . all that we ever do, through just loyalty to our lord, we do to our own great advantage, for truly God will be gracious to him who is duly faithful to his lord."

The supreme authority to which one owes this loyalty is of course that of the king. But, although supreme, the king was not an unfettered despot. Piety and justice were the qualities admired in a good king, and he was also the head of the national household (lord means "loaf-giver"). He was the umpire *par excellence*, the supreme arbitrator under God, the man whose job it was to see that the law and all agreements were kept.

One consequence of this was that crimes committed in his presence were more heinous; there was, or ought to be, a penumbra of peace about his person. So, for instance, if an excommunicated person came into the king's neighbourhood he forfeited his life and goods. And what exactly was "the king's neighbourhood"? It was very accurately defined: it extended on all four sides from the gate of the house where he was "three

miles and three furlongs and the breadth of three acres, and nine
feet and nine spear-hands and nine barley corns." One could not,
of course, be sure when one was within this very nicely defined
sphere of influence, and so it was just as well to keep far away
from the king's neighbourhood if one could not come within it
with safety!

Together with that of the king, the authority of the Church
must be upheld, for it is God's authority. A thief who steals from
a church commits sacrilege and must lose his hand unless the court
allows him *ex gratia* to redeem it by a money payment. The holy-
days of the church must be kept: the twelve days of Christmas;
the 15th February "when Christ conquered the Devil"; the 12th
March, St. Gregory's day, for Gregory had sent St. Augustine to
undertake the conversion of England; Holy Week and Easter
Week; the 29th June, the feast of St. Peter and St. Paul; the week
before the feast of the Assumption of the Blessed Virgin Mary on
the 15th August; the 1st November, All Saints' Day.

Next in gravity to crimes against the king and the Church were
crimes against one's immediate overlord; "with regard to all
classes . . . we ordain that he who plots against the life of his lord
shall forfeit his life to him, and all that he possesses."

Nevertheless, the Saxon codes avoided when possible the actual
taking of life. All sorts of mutilations might be involved, but the
death penalty was comparatively rare. (In nineteenth-century
Britain there were over two hundred capital offences before
Peel's reform of the penal code.) This cautious approach to the
taking of life was due to the influence of the Church. As Archbishop Wulfstan wrote, a hundred and fifty years after Alfred's
time:

> Christians shall not be condemned to death for all too little . . . one
> shall not destroy for a little matter God's own handiwork and His
> own property which He bought at a great price.

Besides treachery to one's lord, the crimes of arson, burglary,
and murder were punishable by death and the confiscation of the
accused's property. To kill a man in a quarrel was not murder,
but to conceal the crime turned it into a capital offence, *slaying in
secret*, which could not be wiped out by money payments.

Lesser penalties were complex. To take only the case of deliberate injury to the hand: loss of a thumb must be paid for with the highest fine; next in importance was the ring finger, followed by the first finger, the middle finger, and, cheapest of all, the little finger. Similarly graded scales applied to other parts of the body —4 shillings for striking out a man's back tooth, 8 shillings for a front one; 30 shillings for an ear; 60 shillings for a nose, and so on.

The principle of graded money payments was also applied to the killing of a man, when this was only homicide and did not deserve capital punishment. Every rank had its *wergild*—the price set upon a man according to his rank. This is in fact one of the clearest ways of distinguishing today to what class of society a man belonged. Thus the wergild of a foreigner, a "Welshman", was less than that of an Englishman, and that of a ceorl was only a sixth of that of a nobleman.

This system of money payments according to rank was one of the two bases of Saxon law. The other was the practice of *compurgation*, or proving one's innocence with the help of a certain number of men who would swear to it. The number of these "oath-helpers" depended on the nature of the charge involved.

A typical Saxon lawsuit took the following form. The plaintiff called the defendant to answer his charge. If the defendant did not appear, he lost his case and if he or his family did not make the necessary compensation for his crime, he became an outlaw. Any one could kill him, and only the king could pardon him.

In most cases it would therefore be better for the defendant to answer the charge. The plaintiff first swore that the charge was genuine and not a false one, due to malice. The defendant was then told how many oath-helpers he must obtain in order to rebut the charge and was given thirty days in which to collect them. At the end of this time the defendant swore: "By the Lord I am guiltless of this deed with which —— charges me." And his oath-helpers swore: "By the Lord, the oath is clean and not false that —— has sworn." If this was done to the satisfaction of the court the case was at an end, for the defendant had cleared himself satisfactorily.

But if the defendant had been caught in the act, or was untrustworthy—not "oath-worthy"—the whole procedure might be reversed and the plaintiff would then bring forward a certain number of oath-helpers to swear to the defendant's guilt.

If the defendant had been proved guilty in this way, or if he had failed to find enough oath-helpers to clear himself of the charge, he might choose to put himself on the judgement of God. The ordeal, as it was called, was under the control of the Church. First the accused fasted for three days and then he went to Mass. In church, before receiving the Sacrament, he was solemnly charged by the Trinity, by his faith, by the cross, and by the Gospel and relics in the church where he was, that he should not take the Sacrament if he were guilty. If the accused continued to maintain his innocence, he might then be subjected to the ordeal in one of three forms, cold water, hot water, or hot iron, at the choice of the plaintiff.

In the ordeal by cold water the accused was given a sip of holy water and then thrown into water—if he floated, the element had rejected him, God had cast him out, and he was guilty. In the ordeal by hot water, a cauldron of water was boiled and when it had been inspected by two men from each side, the accused must plunge his hand in up to the wrist and pick up a stone from the bottom of the cauldron. In serious cases he would have to plunge his arm in to the elbow.

In the ordeal by hot iron, the accused must pick up a piece of iron of one pound weight which had been heated over a fire, and carry it nine feet, measured by the length of his own foot. In a serious case, the iron might be of three pounds weight.

After the ordeal by hot water or iron the accused's hand was bandaged and the wrapping sealed. Three days later the bandage was taken off, and the wound examined "to see whether within the sealed wrapping, it is foul or clean. If anyone breaks any of the conditions, the ordeal shall be a failure, and he shall pay a fine of 120 shillings to the king", as one form of these regulations, dating probably from the reign of Athelstan (925–40), concludes austerely.

A cleric suffered a different form of the ordeal. He swallowed the Host, after praying that it might choke him if he were not telling the truth. Yet the value of this ordeal must have lain in similar factors to those governing the ordeal by iron or water. In an age of faith the man whose conscience was clear might very well heal faster, the cleric might swallow with assurance, while the guilty man would choke or fester. The ordeals were what might be termed psychosomatic tests.

Behind Alfred's dooms, behind the complex structure of wergild and oath-helper, behind the elaborate rituals of the ordeal, lay the comparatively simple machinery for the execution of justice. At its head stood the king, able to judge directly, or to act as a final court of appeal. Most cases were heard first in a local public assembly, the "folk-moot", from which appeal was direct to the king.

Thus, in a law designed to stop feuding, Alfred's code directed the aggrieved man to act as follows: "Let him ride to the ealdorman and ask him for help. If he will not help him, let him ride to the king, before he fights."

The folk-moot assembled once every four weeks under the supervision of a king's reeve, the man who looked after the king's estates in that area, or was in charge of the nearest town. He was responsible for law and order in the area—it was the king's reeve of Dorchester, riding to investigate the situation, who had been cut down by the first Viking raiders in Dorset. In addition there were, of course, church courts under the control of the bishop, and certain private courts granted to landowners by the king. But one rule, says Alfred's code, applies everywhere: "Judge not one judgement for the rich, and another for the poor."

Over all these courts Alfred now proceeded to exercise a close supervision. At the end of his book Asser describes this. There were, he says, frequent quarrels in the moots, but ". . . in the king's presence no wrong would be hidden, for he was a most acute investigator in passing sentence, as he was in all things. He inquired into the judgements given in his absence, throughout almost the whole kingdom, whether they were just or unjust."

If they were unjust, Asser continues, Alfred would find out whether the injustice proceeded from corruption, or ignorance of the law. If the judges were found to be ignorant then "either study the law or give up your office. Such are my commands." Asser paints an amusing picture of the older men "choosing rather laboriously to acquire knowledge of a new kind than to resign their offices" and getting their better-educated sons, or their freedmen, "to recite Saxon Books before them day and night

... lamenting with deep sighs that in their youth they had never attended to such studies." The "Saxon Books" were presumably the Doombooks of the Saxon kings.

If Alfred's own investigations overlooked an injustice, there was always the possibility, already mentioned, of a direct appeal from the folk-moot to the king. A petition to Edward the Elder throws an interesting light on this. It recalls how a dissatisfied plaintiff had come to King Alfred "and the king stood washing his hands within the room" at his manor of Wardour in Wiltshire. And "when he had done washing" he heard the suit. The informality is not considered to be anything remarkable.

Informal or not, Alfred's rule was real. In the next century an Easter Sunday homily declares: "No man can make himself king, but the people has the choice to choose whom they please; but after he is consecrated as king, he then has dominion over the people, and they cannot shake his yoke from their necks." The old men mugging up their lawbooks by candlelight, the king's constant supervision of local justice, his recodification of the laws —all these together provided the basis for the restoration of security. In his translation of Boethius Alfred comments, "Wise men say they can the more easily carry out and maintain their wisdom if their power be absolute over the people subject to them." But Alfred was careful never to overstep the traditional limitations on his power—if he was something of a despot, it was despotism by consent.

Foreign Policy, Religion and Learning

For his Repute, we see him beloved of his own, and
honoured far and near both of his Neighbours and of
strangers.

Sir John Spelman, 1643

STRONG fighting forces and a strong law were the bases of
security and many rulers would have been satisfied with their
establishment. It is part of the greatness of Alfred that he sees the
whole picture—force and faith, learning and law. While the king
was supervising the construction of burhs and the instruction of
judges, he was at the same time concerned for the restoration of
education, of religion, and of diplomatic contacts with foreign
powers.

Beyond Mercia and the Danish settlements there were fragmentary British and Saxon kingdoms, and Alfred was naturally
anxious to establish friendly relations with these. Asser, himself a
Welshman, describes how the British kinglets of Wales looked to
Alfred for support or protection. The rulers of Glamorgan came
under the protection of English Mercia (by this time ruled by
Alfred's brother-in law Ethelred). The principalities beyond
Glamorgan were encouraged to look to Alfred for support against
the sons of Rhodri Mawr—Roderick the Great—who had united
north and central Wales. One of Roderick's own sons, Anarawd
of Gwynedd, came to Alfred's court himself about the year 893.
It is the first recorded visit of a Welsh ruler to a Saxon king.

Beyond Wales to the north there existed by this time in
Lancashire a Norse Viking kingdom and beyond that again another British kingdom, that of the Cymri of Cumberland and
south Scotland. With these shadowy northern rulers Alfred had
no contact, but on the other side of the Pennines he seems to
have controlled for a time the English remnant of the kingdom
of Northumbria. The evidence is scanty, but the fragmentary
asides of later chroniclers, and a handful of coins, suggest that

from 883 to 894 the kingdom was ruled by a Danish protégé of Alfred's, who inscribed on one side of his coins "Cnut Rex" and on the other "Elfred Rex". On this man's death "king Alfred held at his disposal the kingdom of the Northumbrians", but the new king, Siegfred or Siegeferth, withdrew himself from Alfred's overlordship and joined in the last war against him.

In these ways Alfred extended his diplomatic contacts in a tentative way to the north and west. Nowhere north of the Thames was he an absolute ruler, but he was regarded by contemporaries as "the ruler of all Christians in Britain". If the claim seems over-large, he was at least the one fixed point in their world of change.

Asser boasted that foreign embassies were received by Alfred almost continuously. There is clearly more than a little of Asser's Welsh enthusiasm in this picture, but the king's court was certainly visited, at one time or another, by—reading from east to west—Scandinavians, Frisians, Franks, Gauls, Bretons, Welsh and Irish. Alfred for his part was in touch with Flanders, the Papacy, the Patriarch of Jerusalem and—just possibly—with India.

To the south-east of Flanders lay the archiepiscopal city of Rheims, a power in the disintegrating Frankish Empire. Fulk, archbishop of Rheims from 883 to 900, was a political churchman, a great prince-bishop enmeshed in a web of political intrigue. A good man to keep in with. Alfred sent him a present of some pedigree wolf-hounds about the year 885, and asked in return for the scholar-monk Grimbald.

Fulk's reply still exists—as a matter of fact it is the only letter addressed to Alfred of which the full text has survived. The archbishop condescends hugely. He is not impressed by this little Saxon king. There is no doubt in his mind that these uncouth islanders are, consciously or unconsciously, liable to slip into heretical practices. So much is clear behind the distant Latin phrases. He is prepared to "advise and protect" the English. If he allows Grimbald to go—*if* he allows him—then he must be given an English bishopric. Englishmen must come to Rheims too and declare in his presence that they will keep the rules of the Church which "is one, whether it be of Rome or beyond the seas".

In the end, though, Fulk let Grimbald go. He came to England and served Alfred—but he did *not* become a bishop.

Until the aeroplane and the rocket replaced such considerations by larger fears, it had for centuries been a part of British policy to control Flanders, or at least to stop others from controlling it. The area was ruled by an independent count, Baldwin II. And Baldwin's mother was also Alfred's stepmother, the beautiful, young, scandalous Judith who had gone back to France after the death of Alfred's father and from there had made a runaway marriage with the present count's father. This somewhat tenuous link was now strengthened by Alfred as a matter of deliberate policy; here as in so much else the king's action foreshadows later developments—in this case the constant English preoccupation with the Low Countries. His third daughter, Ælfthryth, was married to Count Baldwin II.

At about the time of Alfred's death Baldwin and Ælfthryth clashed with the redoubtable archbishop Fulk, whose lands marched with theirs. There was a long quarrel over the election of an abbot, a quarrel that had disastrous consequences, for in the end Baldwin's followers murdered the obstreperous old archbishop. It was all rather like the story of Thomas Becket, but whereas Henry II did penance for Thomas' murder at Canterbury, Baldwin and his Saxon wife, although pronounced anathema, "cursed in the fruit of their bodies and the fruit of their lands", died unreconciled to the Church.

Alfred himself maintained the traditional friendship between the house of Wessex and the Papacy. No doubt he felt a particular interest in the matter, remembering that he had been twice to the Eternal City as a little boy. In 883 Pope Marinus I sent the *lignum Domini*, a fragment of the True Cross, to Alfred. This may have been a "reward" for the curious incident that had happened a couple of decades earlier, when Rome's portion of the True Cross had been thrown in the mud during a riot, and its reliquary broken in pieces. The precious fragments were recovered and handed back to the Church by an Englishman.

The *Chronicle*, though, links the gift of the *lignum Domini* with Alfred's resumption of the payment made to the Papacy by Offa and by his own father Ethelwulf, the annual gift known later as "Peter's Pence". "Marinus the Pope sent the *lignum Domini* to King Alfred; and the same year Sigelm and Athelstan carried to Rome the alms which the king had vowed to send thither, and also to

St. Thomas in India and to St. Bartholomew," the entry runs. During the eighties these payments seem to have been fairly regular, judging from entries in the Chronicle of this type: "In this year Beocca, ealdorman, carried the alms of the West Saxons and of King Alfred to Rome." (It was by this embassy that Alfred's widowed sister was escorted to Italy.) The tone of the entry suggests an annual payment, and this is borne out by the fact that the absence of an embassy is noted as something to comment on: "In this year there was no journey to Rome, but King Alfred sent two messengers with letters."

In the nineties, however, there is no mention of couriers or embassies. Contact had apparently broken down. Perhaps the last war against the Danes was occupying Alfred, perhaps the scribe was not interested, perhaps the rapid decline in the reputation of the Papacy had something to do with it. Pope Formosus (891–6), (the same Pope whose corpse was later dug up and tried for various crimes) wrote to the Archbishop of Canterbury complaining that "the abominable rites of the pagans have revived in your country, and yet like dumb dogs you keep silent." This can hardly have improved Anglo-Papal relations.

The entry in the *Chronicle* for 882, already quoted, makes the surprising claim that Alfred sent, or at any rate meant to send, an embassy to "St. Thomas in India and to St. Bartholomew". The passage has aroused much debate among historians. It is most unlikely that such an expedition took place. One of Alfred's later writings included a description of the world as known to him, and India is dismissed very cursorily as "the outermost of all countries". It is inconceivable that Alfred would have left it at that if men from England had recently been there.

On the other hand, the relics of St. Bartholomew had been brought to Rome in the ninth century, and the shrine of St. Thomas was at Edessa in the Near East, which was often included in the general term "India". Perhaps Alfred sent gifts to these comparatively accessible shrines, or perhaps the idea of a mission was only a pious hope—or a later pious fiction. It certainly caught the imagination of medieval writers. In the twelfth century William of Malmesbury was quite certain that jewels brought back to Alfred from India could be seen at Sherborne Abbey!

The king was, on at least one occasion, in direct contact with

the Near East. The patriarch of Jerusalem, Elias, was then writing
to all the western rulers to ask for money in order that he might
rebuild his dilapidated churches. Palestine had been in the hands
of the Muslims for two centuries and the Christian congregations
there had fallen on hard times. "Show to us your bowels of kind-
ness," Elias wrote. "If one member suffers, all the members suffer
with it." He went on to bemoan the fact that there was not even
oil for the lamps in the shrines.

Asser says he had seen with his own eyes letters and gifts sent
by the patriarch to Alfred; no doubt Alfred sent his "subscrip-
tion", and he appears also to have asked for medical advice, perhaps about the mysterious pains from which he suffered, for the
East had a well-deserved reputation for reliable medical knowledge. Elias sent the prescriptions and they were added to the
existing Anglo-Saxon recipes. Balsam, he wrote, was good for
coughs, carbuncles, fever, cuts and abrasions. Petroleum could be
taken internally (!) and externally "on a winter's day".

> Treacle is a good drink for all inward tendernesses, and the man
> who follows the instructions here set down, may much help himself.
> On the day on which he shall drink treacle he shall fast until midday,
> and not let the wind blow on him that day; then let him go to the
> bath, let him sit there till he sweat; let him take a cup and put a little
> warm water in it, and then take a little bit of treacle and mingle it
> with the water and strain through some thin cloth; then drink it, and
> let him go to his bed and wrap himself up warm, and so lie till he
> sweat well.

It sounds familiar; a hot bath and keep well wrapped up. One
almost expects to find two aspirins somewhere in the remedy.
This eastern common-sense must have contrasted strangely with
the exotic Anglo-Saxon remedies, "Leechdoms and Wort-
Cunning" as they were called. Consider, for instance, an Anglo-
Saxon remedy for a "fiend-sick" man:

> Collect cockle, lupin, wood betony, cockspur, and hassock-grass,
> wild iris, fennel, lovage, lichen from a church and from a crucifix.
> Place the mixture in clear ale and sing seven Masses over it; put in
> garlic and holy water and put some drops of the mixture into every
> drink that the patient takes.
> Let the patient sing the psalms *Beati immaculati* (Blessed are those

who are undefiled), *Exsurgat* (Let God arise and let His enemies be scattered), and *Salvum me fac, Deus* (Help me, O Lord), and then let him drink of this drink from a church bell (presumably the sacring-bell). After he has drunk, let the priest sing over him *Domine, Sancte Pater Omnipotens.*

Compared with remedies such as this, did the wisdom of the ancient East seem something of an anti-climax to the king?

One is tempted sometimes to forget how great the distances were in Alfred's world, what an immense undertaking an exchange of letters with the patriarch of Jerusalem was. The isolating effect of even quite short distances is brought home to one by an account of the mysterious arrival of a boatload of Irishmen out of the blue. Ireland, only 120 miles or so from Wessex, had been since the Viking invasions almost cut off from England.

> Three Irishmen came to king Alfred in a boat without oars from Ireland. They had stolen away because they were determined to go on a pilgrimage for the love of God—they did not care where they went. They made the boat secretly from two and a half ox-hides, and they put into it provisions for a week. On the seventh day they landed in Cornwall, and set off straight away for Alfred's court. They went on to Rome and they intended to go from there to Jerusalem. Their names were Dubslane, Macbeth and Maelinmun.

This report, drawn partly from the *Chronicle* and partly from Ethelweard's later account, tickles the imagination. The three Irish come out of the mists in their little coracle, pause for a moment in the light of Alfred's court, and then disappear on foot in the direction of the capital of Christendom. The Continent itself was full of Irishmen, refugees from the Vikings, but apparently they did not pass by way of England or these three strangers would hardly have been described in such circumstantial detail.

The restoration of law and order, the establishment of diplomatic contacts with other lands—these activities were, in the king's eyes, valueless without the restoration of religion and learning within the kingdom. Alfred set out the problem as he saw it in his own introduction to the translation of Pope Gregory the Great's *Pastoral Care*, a professional handbook for the use of bishops. The copy sent to bishop Werferth of Worcester is still in existence at Oxford, in the Bodleian Library. At the head of the manuscript it says firmly in capital letters: DEOS BOC SCEAL TO WIGORA CEASTRE (This Book Is For Worcester). A verse prologue, perhaps written by Alfred himself, says:

> King Alfred translated every word of me into English and sent me to his scribes, south and north, and ordered more such to be brought to him that he might send them to his bishops, *for some of them needed it who knew no Latin.*

Then comes the introduction, outlining the problem:

> King Alfred greets Bishop Werferth, with love and friendship in his words.
>
> I want you to know that I often recall what wise men there once were among the English, both religious and secular, and how the kings who ruled them obeyed God and His ministers; they maintained peace and morality and their own authority at home, and at the same time they enlarged their territory abroad; and how they prospered both in war and in wisdom.
>
> I recall too how the religious orders were eager to teach and to learn and to carry out all the services which they owed to God; and how foreigners came here for wisdom and knowledge—now we should have to get them from abroad. So completely had learning fallen away in England that when I came to the throne there were very few to the south of the Humber who could understand their Missals in English, or translate a letter from Latin into English; and I do not think there were many north of the Humber who could do this either. There were so few scholars that I cannot think of even one south of the Thames. . . .
>
> When I recalled all this I remembered too how I saw, before it had all been ravaged and burnt, the churches all over England full of treasures and books, and of God's servants. Yet they had very little idea what was in the books, for they could not understand them because they were not written in their language.

Alfred went on to discuss the importance of translating certain basic works into Anglo-Saxon.

The picture which the king paints of decayed learning and spoiled monasteries is borne out indirectly by the letters of foreigners, such as Pope John VIII (877), Archbishop Fulk, and of Pope Formosus, all of whom assert that the English clergy are too often weak or corrupt.

Asser confirms the general picture:

> For many years the desire for the monastic life had utterly died out among that nation, as indeed it had done among many other nations; and though very many monasteries still remain in existence in that land, yet none keep the rule of that life rightly. I do not know whether this is the result of the invasions of the foreign men which are so frequent both by land and sea; or whether it is the result of the excessive wealth of every kind of that nation; and I think that the latter is much more the cause for the contempt in which the monastic life is held.

Asser makes the important point that the decline in the monastic ideal was not peculiar to England. The next century was to see the reform of the Benedictine rule, based on the monastery of Cluny. Meanwhile, Alfred was not alone in finding the problem insoluble. He did what he could. Many of his laws are specifically designed to enforce a higher standard of morals; for example:

> If anyone takes a nun from a convent without the king's or the bishop's leave, he shall pay 120 shillings, half to the king and half to the bishop. . . .

Alfred founded four monastic communities, at Athelney, Shaftesbury, Winchester and "Nunna-minster". The community at Athelney was a strange mixture of English and Frankish monks, converted heathen, old men, children "later to be raised to the monastic habit", regular clergy and secular clergy. It got away to a bad start. Alfred had placed at its head an expert scholar from Germany, John the Saxon, and two Franks tried to have him murdered. In later centuries Athelney was always overshadowed by the great establishments of Glastonbury and Wells to the north, and engaged in interminable law-suits with the former. By the eighteenth century even the ruins of the foundation had completely disappeared.

Over 350 years ago the piece of work called "Alfred's Jewel" was dug up 2 or 3 miles to the west of Athelney. The jewel (now in the Ashmolean Museum at Oxford) is pear-shaped, 2½ ins. long and about an inch in width. It consists of cloisonné enamel work in green, red and blue, showing a three-quarter length figure with a sceptre in each hand. This is set in a gold rim including the words *Ælfred mec heht gewyrcan*, "Alfred had me made". The narrow end is a gold boar's head, its mouth open to hold, perhaps, a handle. The work is very fine, unequalled in western Europe at the time. Experts disagree as to its function—but in the preface to his edition of Gregory's *Pastoral Care* the king wrote, "I will send one to every see in my kingdom; and in each will be a book-marker" worth three hundred sheep. The jewel may be the head of one of these little sticks, used to keep the place.

At Shaftesbury Alfred set up a religious establishment for women, and placed at its head as abbess his own daughter, Æthelgifu. In the twelfth century William of Malmesbury says he was shown a stone in the chapter-house there which recorded: "In the year of our Lord's Incarnation 880 King Alfred built this city, in the eighth year of his reign"—one of Alfred's line of burhs.

At Winchester Alfred planned two monasteries. He did not live to see their completion, a task which took place in the reign of his son, Edward the Elder. One was the New Minster, later known as Hyde Abbey, where Alfred himself was finally buried. Within fifty years of the Dissolution of Monasteries in Henry VIII's reign, Hyde Abbey had been destroyed, its stones burnt for lime.

"Nunna-minster", the other foundation at Winchester, was St. Mary's Abbey, where Alfred's widow is said to have died. Its site is now occupied by the Abbey Gardens.

The founding of religious houses, the restoration of morality—these were half the business Alfred had set himself and here his efforts were to some extent frustrated by the times in which he lived. The other half of his self-appointed task as restorer of civilization in England was that of reviving learning, and in this he was eminently successful.

Alfred regretted the fact that he had not been educated when young. He now set himself three aims: to restore the general standard of education throughout Wessex; to learn Latin himself; and to translate, or commission translations of, certain books "most necessary for all men to know", thus making available in English a certain minimum amount of basic knowledge. It was a remarkable plan for a Saxon chieftain living on the fringe of civilization to envisage, and—what is even more remarkable—it was to a large extent realized.

The king, again modelling himself on the example of Charles

the Great, determined to make his court the centre of an educational revival, to set up a "Palace School". Einhard, Charles the Great's biographer, writes of his master that "he most zealously cultivated the liberal arts, held those who taught them in great esteem and conferred great honours upon them. He himself took lessons in grammar." He describes how the emperor, the master of western Europe, tried to learn to write, having letter-sheets and books carried on packhorses, wrapped in his bedding-roll when he moved from place to place and, when he could not sleep at night, drawing a tablet from under his pillow and practising the formation of letters. But Charles never really mastered the difficult art of writing; he was too old.

In the decade following the expulsion of the Danes from Wessex, Alfred gathered round him at court a small group of teachers, a "brains-trust". These included his biographer, Asser, without whose *Life* Alfred would be in many ways an indistinct figure.

While there is no doubt as to the existence of Asser himself, there have always been those who have claimed that his book is an eleventh-century forgery. The earliest surviving manuscript was burnt in the early eighteenth century and what is known of it suggests that it was transcribed after the year 1000. In 1904 W. H. Stevenson dealt with the objections that had been raised with regard to the *Life* and appeared to have demonstrated its authenticity. There the matter rested until 1962 when Professor Galbraith reopened the whole matter in his address to the Anglo-American Conference of Historians: "Who wrote Asser's *Life of Alfred*?"

The gist of Professor Galbraith's argument was that the attitude of the writer was such that the work ". . . could not have been written by one man who was alive about another man who was alive. That is the whole point." Alfred was seen as a figure of folk-lore, a neurasthenic invalid. The suspicions raised by the tone of the work would find support in factual errors: a dedication to Alfred as "ruler of all the Christians of the island of Britain"; Asser's claim that Alfred had given him two monasteries not in existence in the ninth century; the Welshman's further claim to have received the bishopric of Exeter—a see that was not in existence before 1050.

If Asser did not write Asser's *Life*, who did? The Professor thought it might perhaps have been written by Leofric, a Welsh-man who was bishop of Exeter in the late eleventh century. It is unlikely that the matter will ever be settled finally one way or the other. Critics of Asser can always point to the admitted in-consistencies in the text. The bishop's supporters will always reply that errors and interpolations crept into later manuscripts, but that the nucleus of the work is by the hand of that Asser who was Alfred's friend and adviser. In the absence of final proof it is safer to accept his account, but to bear in mind that the text has almost certainly been tampered with.

Asser was an elderly Welsh priest from St. David's, Pembroke-shire. He himself describes how, about the year 885, he was per-suaded to visit Alfred—perhaps for a sort of "interview"—at the royal manor of Dene, near Eastbourne.

> I was kindly received by him, and then, among other matters, he begged me eagerly to devote myself to his service and become one of his household, and to leave all that I had west of the Severn. And he promised that he would more than repay me from his own dominions.

There were long negotiations, the upshot of which was that Asser left for home, but promised to return to Alfred's court in six months' time. On the road back to St. David's, however, the

---

TRANSLATION OF ENTRIES IN THE ANGLO-SAXON CHRONICLE REPRODUCED OPPOSITE

877. In this year the great army came to Exeter from Wareham; and the fleet sailed west along the coast and met a great storm at sea, and one hundred and twenty ships perished at Swanage. And King Alfred rode with the fyrd after the mounted army as far as Exeter, and they could not overtake them before they were within the fortress where they might not be reached. And there they gave him hostages, as many as he would have, and swore great oaths, and then kept a good peace. Then in the harvest season the great army went away into Mercia, and apportioned part of it, and gave some to Ceolwulf.

878. In this year in midwinter after Twelfth night the great army came stealthily to Chippenham, and over-ran the land of the West-Saxons and occupied it, and drove overseas many of the people, and conquered most of the rest, and forced them to submit, save King Alfred, and he with a small band of followers went with difficulty to the woods and the fastnesses of the moors.

Welshman fell ill with a fever and was forced to remain at Caer-went for over a year. The pertinacious Alfred sent messengers to find out what had become of him. Asser replied that he would come when he could, and eventually he did return to court, prob-ably some time in the year 887, having made an arrangement with the King by which he should be allowed to divide his time equally between Wessex and Pembroke, spending six months at each place. In fact it was eight months before Alfred gave him his first leave.

St. Martin's Day (11th November) was a red-letter day in Alfred's life in more senses than one, for it was on that day, in the year 887, that Asser began to teach the Saxon king the elements of translation from Latin, choosing phrases and sentences from the Latin version of the Bible, the Vulgate. To judge from later events, it looks as though it took Alfred about five years (887-92) to become a competent Latin scholar.

Asser describes in some detail this seminal moment in the king's education. "We were," says Asser, "sitting together in the king's room, as usual, talking of this and that." Can one detect a hint of smug satisfaction, an implication that by this time they were familiar friends?

Alfred listened very intently to a passage that Asser was reading to him, then he pulled out from the folds of his tunic a book con-taining the Offices for the Day, the psalms, and some miscel-laneous prayers he had heard when he was a boy. "He said he always carried this book about with him." The king asked Asser to copy the quotation that had just been read to him into the book. Asser says he gave praise to God—"silently, of course"—and took the book. But there was no room left in it. "Wherefore I made a little delay."

The king urged him to hurry up and write quickly. Then Asser suggested that he had better write the quotation on a separate parchment.

"Perhaps," said Asser, "we shall find one or two other extracts that you will want to have written down. If that does happen, we shall be glad we have kept them apart."

Alfred agreed, and Asser began straight away on the king's commonplace book. "The first entry in it was the passage he had just asked for, and on that same day I added three more; and

9

from that time we talked together every day, so that the sheet became full. . . . Now when that first quotation was copied, he was eager at once to read, to translate into Saxon, and then to teach others."

Asser says very correctly that Alfred's education had got under way "by divine inspiration", but it is clear that he felt the real credit was his. Eventually the commonplace book became "almost as large as a psalter". Alfred called it his *Enchiridion*, or *Handbook*, because he kept it at hand day and night, and he told Asser it gave him great comfort to read it.

Alfred's *Handbook* has disappeared. There is just a hint that it was still known in the twelfth century. It is exciting to play with the fancy that it is still in existence, waiting to be rediscovered . . . that one might know just which were the quotations that held his interest. . . . Perhaps, on the other hand, the book never existed, and is a fabrication of the pseudo-Asser?

After Asser had been eight months in Wessex, and when he must have been wondering how much longer he would have to wait for his holiday at St. David's, the king suddenly sent for him. It was Christmas Eve. Alfred's Christmas presents to Asser were the properties of Congresbury and Banwell to the north of the Mendips. There was particular delicacy in the choice of these two places as a gift to a Welshman, for they were both dedicated to St. Congar, a Celtic saint well-respected in Wales. Alfred also gave him permission to go home and visit his friends.

Asser came back to Wessex and settled there; he was made a bishop with control over the western part of the kingdom, based on Exeter, and when he finally died ten years after his patron, he had been for some time bishop of Sherborne. He does not give us much information about his own later life, and his *Life* of Alfred stops, disappointingly, about the year 892, just when the king's last war against the Danes was beginning. It would have been valuable to have a picture of Alfred the man of war to set beside Asser's portrait of Alfred the scholar.

Asser is Alfred's Einhard, Alfred's Boswell, though his *Life* will not quite stand up to the comparison. He is only concerned to show us Alfred as a Christian, faced with great danger from the heathen, successfully defeating them at the battle of Ethandun and then reorganizing the state of Wessex. There is a tendency to stress the king's spiritual outlook and religious motives, not unnatural in the circumstances but resulting in a distorted portrait of Alfred, and one that is certainly responsible for the Victorian milk-and-water view of the king. Asser is inclined to under-rate, or even omit altogether, the work of Alfred's brothers, and also to overdramatize situations. It has been suggested that he wrote the book with one eye on the home market, attempting to provide for Cornish and Welsh readers information about this king who was so successfully resisting the new enemy. But when all these reservations have been made, it remains true that Asser's *Life*—if genuine—provides a unique and living picture of the king.

There were other teachers besides Asser at Alfred's Palace School. From Mercia the King drew four scholars: the priests Athelstan and Werwulf; Werferth, created bishop of Worcester in 873; and Plegmund, Alfred's own "mass-priest" (royal chaplain) who was created Archbishop of Canterbury in 890. The out-spoken Archbishop Fulk of Rheims—who, as has been seen already, took a dark view of the religious conditions in England—congratulated Alfred on this appointment. Plegmund, he wrote, is "busy cutting away with the sword of his tongue that most perverse following of heathen error still left among the English . . . errors deep-rooted in your nation."

Asser and the four Mercians were home-grown products. From overseas Alfred obtained the scholars Grimbald and John. John was a Saxon from West Germany—"a most energetic man, an expert scholar and writer, skilful in many other arts," was how Asser described him.

Perhaps John the Saxon was *too* energetic. Alfred made him abbot of his pet foundation at Athelney, and the appointment had unfortunate consequences. It was a mixed community, many of the monks being Frankish refugees. Perhaps it was difficult to "staff" such a damp, isolated place, perhaps the two races found one another already antipathetic. Whatever the reasons, the Saxon abbot and the Frankish community were soon at cross-purposes. Before long a priest and a deacon, both Franks, had bribed a couple of Frankish servants to murder the abbot.

These men, armed with stolen swords, tiptoed towards John as he prayed before the altar one night. The plan was to kill him and then leave the body before the house of a local harlot "as if he had been slain whilst on a visit to her". The two assailants wounded John before anyone could come to his help, but not before he had put up a brave fight for, Asser says, he knew how to defend himself and would have made a fine fighter if he had not chosen a better calling. John's cries eventually brought the monks to the doors of the church, and the would-be murderers escaped into the wilds, leaving the abbot half dead.

John recovered from his wounds. The servants and the instigators of the crime were caught and put in prison "where", Asser concludes curtly, "by various tortures they came to a disgraceful end; let us now return to our narrative".

The other foreigner, Grimbald, reached England about the same time that Asser arrived at Alfred's court. He came from the abbey of St. Bertin, near the modern town of St. Omer in the Pas-de-Calais. Grimbald was already an old man of seventy when archbishop Fulk allowed him to go to Wessex. He was settled in a little church community at Winchester and later he became head of Alfred's New Minster there. He helped the king with his Latin and no doubt told him stories of his life at St. Bertin and of the days when a bastard son of Alfred's hero Charles the Great had been his abbot.

It was a quiet end to a life that had not always been so peaceful. The north-west angle of Europe, where the abbey was situated, had been heavily raided. In 861 St. Bertin had been sacked by the Vikings and those four monks who had not fled to the surrounding woods were found by their colleagues when these came back, tortured to death. Now Grimbald lived gently in Hampshire till his own death on 8th July 901. The exact date is known, for the English came to regard him as a saint, and kept his feast on that day.

These, then, were the members of the "brains-trust" that Alfred gathered together. Not great names, but good scholars, who could help him to do a satisfactory job of work that would endure. If Sir John Spelman is over-optimistic in his comment on the effect of Alfred's educational policy when he writes that he ". . . in a short time brought it to pass that Learning and Civility, which formerly had been in Contempt, became the only Thing in request and generally desired of every Man", his comment on the men themselves is a fitting one; "wheresoever the king could light on any Men for his purpose, by all the means he could he procured them to come over to him, and help him in setting again on foot the Knowledge of Letters here in this Land: and such was his exceeding Liberality in the Entertainment of them, as that, notwithstanding their Scarcity, he soon furnished himself with very choice Men, of whom there are some that are to this Day remembered unto us."

A New Frontier (878–86)

If a man be slain, whether an Englishman or a Dane, we
shall all place the same value on his life.
Alfred's Treaty with Guthrum

ALFRED, in the middle years of his reign, was primarily concerned with strengthening the defences, re-establishing good
government, and restoring what Erasmus would have called
"good letters", but he was never able to concentrate all his attention on these problems. He was never free from the Viking
pressure. There was no great war but there was a series of probing
raids on the part of the enemy, and a serious crisis in the middle
eighties that resulted in the division of England and the establishment of a new civilization on the farther side of the new frontier.

After their defeat at Ethandun, Guthrum and his Danes had
wintered at Cirencester. Then in the spring they had left the west
—never to return—and moved back to East Anglia, to the area
where they had landed fourteen years earlier. There they divided
the land amongst themselves, the third and final Danish partition of English territory.

In 881 the *Chronicle* records a naval battle in which Alfred's
new ships engaged four Danish vessels—hit-and-run raiders of the
old type, who had perhaps not heard of the renaissance of Saxon
power. If so, they must have had a sharp surprise: two ships were
captured, two fled.

In 885 Alfred received a more alarming reminder that it was
not only the Danes already in England who might overthrow
him. The Viking horde that had wintered at Fulham in the year
of Ethandun and had then sailed away to try its luck on the Continent, suddenly returned and besieged Rochester, digging an
encampment for themselves outside the town. Once again, however, the new spirit that was abroad in Wessex manifested itself

Rochester did not tamely surrender, an action which might have given the enemy an impregnable base of the sort that Reading had provided in the former war. Nor did the men of Kent buy off their tormentors, as they had done twenty years earlier. Instead the burh settled down to endure a siege, confident that the king would come to its aid.

The confidence of the Rochester garrison was not misplaced. Alfred marched rapidly east with the new model army. The Danes were driven back to their ships, their horses—Kentish stock which they had as usual rounded up for transport—were recaptured, and some of those who escaped were glad to beat a rapid retreat to the more easily lootable Continent.

> And so, having made but a short stay there, and only lightened themselves of their Baggage, they are yet once again sent over Sea, and forced a second time to entertain themselves in France.

So far, so good. But Alfred was disturbed to discover that the arrival of their compatriots had roused the barely quiescent Danes in East Anglia. Some of the new invaders had not returned to the mainland of Europe but, having given hostages for good behaviour, had spent the summer in Guthrum's kingdom. From there they launched two raids across the Thames into the densely wooded district of Surrey, while a third larger attack was mounted from the trouble-makers' new base at Benfleet in Essex.

That Guthrum was giving the raiders sanctuary was bad, but much worse was the fact that there was plenty of evidence that his men were helping the newcomers. The Chronicler had no illusions on this point—"the Danish army in East Anglia broke peace with Alfred the king," he wrote.

Once more the real danger was from the land, not from the sea. Like Red Indians, the Danes possessed a fighting spirit easily aroused, but quenched with difficulty. It was clear that something must be done and done quickly, if East Anglia were not to become simply an immense fortified camp over against Wessex. Guthrum must be reminded of his defeat at Ethandun, his christening at Wedmore and all that those two events implied. Then a clear frontier must be established, guaranteed by the two leaders.

Thus Alfred reasoned, and in the light of this reasoning one can understand his actions during the years 885-6. First he sent his new fleet from Kent to harry the coast of Suffolk and Essex. At the mouth of the River Stour they surprised sixteen Viking ships, captured them all and killed their crews. Unfortunately on the homeward journey, the ships heavy with booty, they ran into the remainder of the Viking fleet, perhaps alerted by the news of events in the Stour estuary. "They ply their oars, they remove their sails, their arms glitter on the conquered waves," said Alfred's descendant Ethelweard, and this time the Danish-men got the victory.

If the outcome of the actions at sea was nicely balanced, on land Alfred now held the initiative. In 886 he achieved a dramatic success.

> "King Alfred occupied London, and all the English race submitted to him which was free from the control of the Danes; and then he entrusted the town to the keeping of Ethelred the ealdorman."

London was not then the capital of England. England did not exist, nor did the concept of a fixed capital. In Roman times the city had been a great port and the nodal point of the Roman road system. The geographical excellence of its position ensured its survival when the Romans left. Nevertheless, from that time until its renaissance under Alfred, its history is elusive. It appears and disappears in the surviving records like a Cheshire cat. Bede said that in the early seventh century the city was full of heathen, presumably Saxon squatters. By Bede's own time in the eighth century she had again become, in his own words, "the market of many nations".

There are hints that Alfred had besieged the city a few years before, but it is quite possible it had been in Viking hands continuously for fifteen years, ever since Halfdan had taken it from the Mercians in 872 and, setting up his quarters there, had struck his own coins. Now it was in Saxon hands once more and Alfred encouraged rebuilding within the city. London as a trading centre soon regained any importance it may have lost during the Viking occupation. Three years later the Bishop of Winchester, for instance, was granted a court in an old stone building there for the purpose of buying and selling.

The capture of London, probably the largest settlement in

Viking lands, set a visible seal on Alfred's natural position as king of England. Now was the time, he felt, to make a definite and permanent settlement with Guthrum and the Danes of East Anglia. The resulting agreement, known as the Treaty of Alfred and Guthrum, delimits exactly the respective spheres of influence of Dane and Saxon.

Clearly the treaty was not imposed by Alfred. It is an arrangement reached for their mutual benefit between two equal powers. In effect they say, "we have got to learn to live together, and this is the best way we can manage to do it".

The frontier was carefully defined: "up the Thames, and then up the River Lea to its source, then straight to Bedford, and then up the River Ouse to Watling Street" (now largely represented by the modern main road A5). Beyond the junction with Watling Street the Danish-held territory was probably not under Guthrum's control, but under that of an independent kingdom in Leicestershire. In effect, however, as later wars were to show, Alfred controlled Mercia south of Watling Street right up to its northern terminus at Chester.

In terms of modern counties, Alfred had recognized Guthrum's right to rule over Essex, Suffolk, Norfolk, Cambridgeshire, Huntingdonshire and parts of Bedfordshire and Hertfordshire. In terms of Saxon politics, he had abandoned to the foreigner East Anglia and a large part of Mercia.

The interests of the Saxons thus handed over to Danish rule are carefully safeguarded in the central clauses of the treaty, which fix a relative scale of wergilds for the two races. The details are not important, but what is immensely significant is the fact that Danes and Saxons are to be treated on the basis of equality; though the wergilds seem to be weighted in favour of the Danes. "If a man be slain, whether an Englishman or a Dane, we shall all place the same value on his life," runs a key clause.

The frontier was no mere line on a map. Other clauses forbade free migration from one territory to the other. Trade between the two areas was strictly regulated: it must take place before witnesses, and traders must be prepared to give hostages for their good behaviour. Something of an Iron Curtain was set up; border-raids and border-feuds must be prevented as far as possible or they would give rise to "incidents".

The peace lasted for seven years. With its signing the old heathen raider Guthrum, now a respectable—or at least nearly respectable—Christian ruler, passes out of Alfred's story. He died in 890, and was probably buried at Hadleigh in Suffolk. The *Chronicle* treats his memory with respect: "Guthrum the northern king died, whose baptismal name was Athelstan: he was king Alfred's godson. . . ." Later writers were not so generous. William of Malmesbury, writing in the twelfth century, saw Guthrum in these terms:

> "as the Ethiopian cannot change his spots, he domineered over these tributary provinces with all the haughtiness of a tyrant."

The Alfred–Guthrum treaty accepted the partition of Mercia. From the point of view of local Saxon politics, this could have been dynamite. Relations between Mercia and Wessex had not been good in the past, although they had improved with the marriage of Alfred's sister to king Burhred. More recent though, were Burhred's flight, the collapse of Mercia, and the treachery of Ceolwulf "the foolish king's thegn", who had allowed himself to be manœuvred into the position of a Mercian quisling. Some modern historians have suggested that he performed a valuable service to his country by maintaining the structure of government, but that was not how he appeared to contemporaries, and the argument is reminiscent of Laval's defence of his collaboration with the Germans.

Ceolwulf disappears from history after the year 875. He had served his purpose. Later chroniclers suggest suitable ends for him, death in poverty or, in one instance, a more horrible fate, but there is no real evidence. He may have survived into the eighties. When the mists clear again in 886, Mercia is being ruled by an ealdorman, Ethelred, who is in touch with Alfred.

In effect Mercia, which had once rivalled Wessex, now depended on Alfred's army, and on Alfred's skill and reputation, to maintain its freedom. The king showed his statesmanlike qualities in his handling of this prickly situation. Mercia was allowed to enjoy a sort of "dominion status". When Alfred recovered London, he was scrupulously careful to return the city to Ethelred. Coins minted at Oxford, Gloucester and London—all Mercian towns—bear Alfred's name, but the country kept its own witan, its own privy council. About the time of the treaty with Guthrum, perhaps in the next year (887), Alfred sent his eldest daughter, Æthelflæd, to Mercia to become the ealdorman's wife. The diplomatic marriage was a success. The Mercians accepted the loss of half their kingdom to the Danes. Alfred and Ethelred worked well together in the later wars, Ethelred's position being that of a sort of viceroy, second in command (*subregulus*). Æthelflæd was young enough to be Ethelred's daughter, and after her husband's death she was recognized as "Lady of the Mercians". Under this unique title she ruled her adopted country until her own death at Tamworth on 12th June 918, building fortresses, capturing Derby and Leicester from the resurgent Danes, and in general showing that she had inherited a fair share of her father's gifts.

By the king's treaty with Guthrum a new state had been created, the Danelaw. Alfred's device was to accept the hard fact that the Vikings could not be driven from the island, and then to determine to what extent and within what limits co-existence was possible. The treaty was from this point of view an agreement by which the rights of the already conquered Saxons were safe-guarded, while at the same time the Viking overlords and their free peasant followers were confined to the further side of a clearly defined frontier.

Since the Romans left in the fifth century there had always been frontiers within southern England. Now there was a new one, running in general diagonally across England from just north of London to modern Liverpool. It was a frontier that cut across old divisions like the Roman Fosse Way.

Beyond this border a different way of life appeared, a change not fully apparent by the time of Alfred's death, but a consequence of his work. It was different, but not so changed that one can easily describe in what the difference lay, yet both the difference and the ambiguity were results of Alfred's policy. The Danes have left a mark in place-names, in personal names and in dialect that has survived to the present day.

The new civilization developed in ways neither purely Saxon nor purely Viking, but certainly distinct from that of free Saxon England. In later centuries this area might pass under the control of Saxon kings, or Vikings such as Canute might rule over Saxon England, but these were political changes—changes of rulers. In spite of these vicissitudes the area defined in Alfred's treaty, together with the district of Viking settlement in the north of England, retained a character of its own. It was still possible to say of England at the time of the battle of Hastings, two centuries after Alfred's days, that the all-important line of regional differences "was that which separated Wessex and English Mercia, jointly, from the Danelaw".

It was Alfred's treaty that had called this new area, the Danelaw, into existence. The boundary recognized the existing balance of power. There were Danes living outside the Danelaw to the west, just as there were Saxons to the east, but the line had the merit of being easy to recognize and follow in the days before maps existed—nobody could cross a river by mistake!

The Danelaw was the area where the Danes lived, whoever ruled over them. It was not a homogeneous unit; there was a good deal of cultural give-and-take. The earliest extant private letters in Old English express disapproval of the way in which Saxons are aping Danish customs: "... it is a shame for all of you to give up the English customs of your fathers and to prefer the customs of heathen men, who grudge you your very life; you show thereby that you despise your race and your forefathers with these bad habits, when you dress shamefully in Danish wise. . . ."

It is worth having a closer look at the characteristics which this region developed in later years, since their existence was a consequence of Alfred's actions. There were four areas of Danish control, differing in some ways from one another. In the north the southern half of the old kingdom of Northumbria led an independent existence with its capital at York, from Halfdan's army settlement of 876 till the expulsion of Eric Bloodaxe in 954, its boundaries corresponding approximately to those of the modern county of Yorkshire.

To the south of the Yorkshire Danes, between the Rivers Humber and Welland, lay the area of the Five Boroughs, controlled from the Danish centres of Stamford, Leicester, Derby, Nottingham and Lincoln. These were probably set up about 877 after Alfred had forced the Danish army to evacuate Exeter and move back into Mercia. All except the first later became the centres of new counties. They passed under Saxon control for a time in the middle of the tenth century, but had perhaps the most foreign character of all the Danish settlements.

East Anglia had been settled by Guthrum's army when they withdrew from Western Mercia in the year after Ethandun. The Danes in this area were temporarily subdued by Alfred's son, Edward the Elder, but the area remained one of those strongly coloured by Danish manners.

The last area of Danish settlement was an amorphous area in the south-east Midlands—the later counties of Northampton-shire, Rutland, Huntingdonshire, Cambridgeshire, Bedfordshire, Hertfordshire, Buckinghamshire and Middlesex. Some parts of this area lay partially or wholly outside the political Danelaw, but within what may be called the "social Danelaw"—the area affected by Danish custom. Thus the legal codes of these parts, lying on the Saxon side of the frontier, show clear traces of Scandinavian influence, while in Hertfordshire, also on the Saxon side of the boundary, was Dacorum Hundred, "the Hundred of the Danes".

Indeed it is largely through the distribution of placenames that the limits and to some extent the density of Scandinavian settlement can be deduced, and a name on a twentieth-century signpost is often one of the clearest indications of the ways in which the men of the Danelaw continue to affect our lives today. Now the derivation of placenames is notoriously tricky stuff to handle. The Archbishop of Canterbury has a palace at Lambeth; *beth* in Hebrew means the house of God . . . there is, of course, no connection between these two facts. Yet amateur guesswork has produced derivations just as extraordinary, and even common-sense is not much help. Bridgwater in Somerset seems a cut-and-dried case, the bridge is there and so is the water, but in fact the name was originally "bridge Walter". The only safe rule is to discover the earliest surviving form of the name, which may be very different from that in use today.

Nevertheless, there are certain general statements that one can make about Scandinavian placenames which, in any particular case, are more likely to be right than wrong. If you live in the Danelaw, or are passing through it, they will provide a rough guide to Danish settlements.

The commonest Danish endings of placenames are -*by*, -*thorp*, and -*toft*, in that order. *By*, as in Whitby, for instance, has the approximate meaning of village. *Thorp* (e.g. Easthorpe in Nottinghamshire) represents a smaller or secondary settlement—an outlying farm or hamlet. (This is a dangerous ending to generalize about, since there was an identical Saxon word with an identical meaning! Within the Danelaw *thorp* is more likely to be Danish than Saxon, but one must be very wary.) The third in the trio, *toft* or farmhouse (e.g. Lowestoft) is quite safe.

Beyond this, the amateur cannot safely go. "Danes Court" in Kent, for instance, looks straightforward enough, but in fact it is derived from the Saxon word "dean" (a valley). It is always safest to look up one's guesses in a dictionary of placenames.

In the hands of the specialist, however, the distribution of placenames can reveal a great deal. Thus, if names which can be conclusively shown to have ended in Scandinavian -*by* are added up, one gets the following table:

Lincolnshire	260
Yorkshire, North Riding	150
,, West ,,	58
Leicestershire	58
Yorkshire, East Riding	42
Nottinghamshire	21
Norfolk	21
Northamptonshire	18
Derbyshire	10

Yorkshire, Lincolnshire, Leicestershire—these were precisely the areas particularly involved in the Great Army settlement carried out by the Danes.

Not all Danish colonies were on new sites. Sometimes they took over an existing Saxon village and renamed it. In the nature of things, one cannot be sure how often this happened, but there are sufficient known examples to support the statement. Thus the Danes changed the name of the Saxon settlement of Northworthig ("north homestead") to Deoraby ("village with a deer park") which eventually became Derby. A city whose name has changed out of all recognition is York—and it was the Scandinavians who gave the decisive twist to the name, as the following list of changes shows:

Eboracum   (Roman)
Eoforwick   (Saxon)
Yorwik   (Viking)

Placenames also provide some clues to the social structure of the Danelaw. In the area controlled by the Five Boroughs, for instance, the land was divided for administrative purposes into units called "sokes". The manor of Bolingbroke—a Saxon name —was the centre of one of these. But twelve of the nineteen villages dependent on Bolingbroke bore Scandinavian names. What had apparently happened was that the Danish colonists had been settled in groups to which the less important leaders usually gave their names. while the chief who controlled them took for himself the chief English settlement in the district.

The distribution of personal names can also give some hints about Danish settlement. Such lists as exist date from long after Alfred's time, and all the evidence suggests that the Scandinavian language was still being spoken in parts of the north at the beginning of the twelfth century. Pre-conquest lists show a proportion of Scandinavian names in South Yorkshire of 66 per cent, in north Cambridgeshire of 50 per cent, and in Northamptonshire of 33 per cent. These were lists of important men only and the proportions among peasants may have been quite different; but lists of Danelaw peasants exist for the twelfth century and in them Danish names can be counted by hundreds in Yorkshire and Lincolnshire—the very areas in which the evidence of placenames also indicates Danish settlement.

So what can be learnt from names suggests a reasonably heavy and persistent Danish colonization, at least in some parts of the Danelaw.

The personal names in the lists are heavy and gnarled and grim as the Vikings themselves: Haward and Agmund, Aszur and Byrgher; Ase, Aki and Thori, Ofram "the lazy" and Mole "the dull"; even the feminine names are weighty, Ingirith, Siggerith, and Jorild.

Men's names are in every sense personal and persistent things, and some Norse examples have survived, tamed and anglicized, as modern surnames, linking today directly with the Danelaw of Alfred's time. Allgood, Fathers, Lawman, and Tunney have come straight from the old Danish. Scandinavian names possibly but not certainly from the Danelaw include Bond, Brothers, Foot, Grave, Haldane, Harold, Knott, Coleman, Simmonds, Storey and Westman. Modern Christian names derived from the Scandinavian include: Eric, Harold, Ingrid, Ivor, Olaf, Ralph and Ronald.

The Saxons and Danes shared a considerable common vocabulary—some words were identical, many others were fairly similar in form or general meaning. These similarities naturally helped the process of assimilation, but they have also made it impossible to be dogmatic about the exact extent to which the Scandinavians affected the growth of our everyday vocabulary.

Some common words of which one can be fairly certain include the verbs: call, die, drown, hit, scare, scrape, scream, scrub, scowl, take, thrive and want. Nouns in daily use are: fellow, gate, husband, knife, root, skin, skill, sky, skull, Thursday, window, anger, and egg. Adjectives include: happy, ill, low, loose, meek, odd, rotten, ugly, wrong. Some modified words, similar in Saxon and Scandinavian are: birth, bread, dream, get, give, sister. An example of the kind of thing that happened is provided by the word "earl". This started out in life as the Saxon "eorl" (nobleman, or even just "brave man") and then took over the meaning of the Norse word "jarl" (underking).

There is no pattern in the kind of words affected by the Scandinavians, and this random impact is in itself significant. It implies that Scandinavian culture must have been technically neither very superior nor very inferior to that of the Saxons.

The Danes introduced certain administrative and social changes. They used for many purposes a duodecimal system, with a strong emphasis on groupings of three and four. Thus their currency table ran as follows: sixteenpence in one ora; eight ora in one mark; one hundred and twenty ora in one "hundred" of silver. Yorkshire and Lindsey were both divided into areas known as "thirdings"—a division that has survived in Yorkshire in the form of "Ridings". In their own country the Scandinavians also used "fourthings", "sixings", and "eightings".

The Saxon shire was divided into hundreds: in the Danelaw these were overlaid, or replaced, by the "wapentake". Originally this was the name of an assembly at which free men turned up with their weapons ("weapontake"), but eventually it became by transference the name of the area from which the assembly was drawn. Within the Danelaw the counties of Cumberland, Durham, Lancashire, Yorkshire, Cheshire, Lincolnshire, Nottinghamshire, Leicestershire, Derbyshire, Rutland and Northamptonshire, were all subdivided in this way.

From the codes of law a certain amount of rather disconnected information can be gleaned. In the Danelaw, for instance, the compensation paid to a lord for the murder of one of his men varied in accordance with *the dead man's rank*. In Saxon England the sum paid varied with *the rank of the overlord*. It looks from this suspiciously as though a lord's man had what one might term a greater individuality in the Danelaw, while in Wessex the seriousness of homicide depended on the importance of the man whose property had been destroyed.

From a Northumbrian code of law there comes an interesting scale of charges for murder, the wergild payable to relatives, which gives one a guide to the relative importance of the various classes. Incidentally the wergild is expressed in units of three silver pennies (*thrysma*)—another instance of the use by the Danes of a duodecimal notation:

Ceorls	266
Thegns	2,000
King's reeves	4,000
Ealdormen and Bishops	8,000
Archbishops and King's sons	15,000
King	30,000

The wergild for slaying a king is explained as being due half for the injury done to the king as a man, and half for the affront given to the royal office of kingship—to the abstract constitutional fiction of "the Crown", a surprisingly sophisticated conception.

The Danes came as pirates, but they stayed as farmers—and very successful they were. The wealthiest and most densely populated counties at the time of the Norman Conquest were Suffolk, Norfolk and Lincolnshire—all of them situated in the Danelaw. There is evidence too that the Danes settled heavily in marginal lands that the Saxons had not developed, such as the agriculturally "difficult" wooded areas of north-west Nottinghamshire.

Yet although the settlement in these specialized areas was dense, the bulk of the Danish immigrants received land in districts that had been farmed by the Saxons for centuries. Over the greater part of the Danelaw one must picture a minority of foreign settlers working the land with the help of a large Saxon population. So it is hardly surprising that the existing pattern of agriculture was little affected by the Danes, especially as the Saxon methods of farming were not very different from those they had been used to in Scandinavia.

Farming technique might not change, but methods of landholding did. Under the Saxons the ploughland belonging to a village was divided into hides, each hide containing—in theory at least—four yardlands. The yardland represented the amount of land that would support one peasant household.

Throughout the southern midlands this system went on unchanged, even in those areas containing many Danish placenames and therefore presumably occupied by the foreigners. But in adjoining East Anglia there is no longer any trace of a regular system of holdings of this sort, and in Lincolnshire, beyond the River Welland, the hides and yardlands give place to different units of measurement, ploughlands and oxgangs, eight of the latter to each ploughland. The plough team was an eight-ox one. The ploughland represented the amount of land such a team could work during the year, and the oxgang the contribution of one man, one household, to the team.

Yet when all is said and done even these changes were slow and partial. Peasants are notoriously conservative and in Yorkshire "hides" and "oxgangs" were being used more or less indiscriminately in the eleventh century.

At the base of the social pyramid in the Danelaw as elsewhere were the slaves—a considerable number of them, but even so apparently not so large as in other parts of the country. Above them was the social group that most clearly distinguished the Danelaw from Saxon England, the "sokemen", who formed what has been termed a peasant aristocracy.

In East Anglia *Domesday Book* records a complication in the social structure. There are two types of free men: the "sokemen" and the "free men". In Norfolk the two groups were evenly divided—5,000 of each—while in Suffolk there were only 1,000 sokemen to 8,000 free men.

There was nothing like these sokemen in the Saxon set-up. Two hundred years after Alfred's day their presence is recorded in every county in the Danelaw. There were 11,000 of them in Lincolnshire, 2,000 in Leicestershire, and over 1,500 in Nottinghamshire. They were not rich—amongst them a holding of 40 acres was a considerable estate—but they *were* free.

Each of these independent peasant proprietors was a lord's man, but his duties were light. He had to help his lord at the critical seasons of seedtime and harvest—to attend his lord's law-court, and to pay him a small sum each year. In all other ways this peasant aristocrat was his own master. He paid his other taxes direct to the king, and he could alienate his land if he wanted to. It was natural that in this way the Danelaw should differ from Saxon England. It would be unrealistic to expect that Viking raiders, after years of fighting in a strange land should, when they at last settled down in that land, accept a subordinate position to that of the chief who had recently led them in battle. He might be accepted as their economic superior, but be recognized only to a very limited extent as their legal overlord.

The Last War (892–6)

By the mercy of God the Great Army had not altogether broken the English race.

Anglo-Saxon Chronicle, 896

THE middle years of Alfred's reign passed, as has been seen, in the restoration of law and civilization, and in the repelling of relatively minor raids, while in the Danelaw the former pirates were learning, or remembering, how to be peasant farmers. Alfred was not destined, however, to live out his reign in peace. The last decade was occupied by another great war against the Danes. The danger was not as great as in the first years of the king's reign, but the scope of operations was more widespread, and Alfred had to fight hard to keep what he had saved. In this new crisis his military and naval reorganization stood him in good stead.

In 891 one of the roving Danish armies that were terrorizing the Continent—it was the same one that had wintered at Fulham in 879 and been repelled from Rochester in 884—was badly mauled in Flanders. The River Dyle near Louvain was filled with dead Norsemen and sixteen royal standards were captured. Even the activities of raiders are subject to the law of diminishing returns. Flanders had become too hot to hold the Danes, too poor to support them. They must look elsewhere for a living.

These were the circumstances in which, in the late autumn of 892, a new Great Army sailed from Boulogne for England.

The Great Army was not the only force that was planning to attack Wessex. At much the same time that it was leaving Boulogne a smaller fleet of eighty ships, led by a famous Viking, Hæsten, was planning a descent on the Thames estuary. As a young man Hæsten had taken part in the great Mediterranean raid of 859–61 when a large fleet of ships had passed the Pillars of Hercules and attacked the coasts of Spain, Provence and northern

Italy as far as the neighbourhood of Pisa. More recently he had himself killed Count Robert the Strong, father of the king of France. This formidable man was now sailing to cross swords with Alfred.

The movements of the two fleets make it almost certain that they were acting in unison. Hæsten landed his men on the north coast of Kent at Milton, near Sittingbourne. At the same time the Great Army, with a fleet of about 250 ships, was sailing up the River Lymne, on the south Kentish coast. The strategy was clearly to detach this part of Wessex by a pincer movement and set up there an independent kingdom like the one in East Anglia on the north side of the Thames estuary—an area from which the new men might, incidentally, expect to receive support. If they succeeded, the whole of the east coast from Tees to Hastings would be in their hands.

The attack seems to have taken Wessex completely by surprise. The ships sailing up the Lymne came upon Saxon ceorls in the very act of digging a fort, part of Alfred's system of burhs. As already mentioned, they took over the unfinished work for themselves, and dug themselves in at Appledore. Between the two Danish armies there stretched the great wood, Andredsweald, 120 miles long "or more", says the *Chronicle*—and 30 miles across. Now only the name the Weald survives. The trees were cut down to provide fuel for ironworks in the days when Sussex was the Black Country of England.

The Danish armies fanned out from their two bases, one on either side of the great forest, and began plundering to build up stores for the winter.

What was Alfred doing meanwhile? This is a question that cannot always be answered during the nineties; the course of the war is illuminated, fitfully, in detail, but only partially. The *Chronicle* is like a torch, describing carefully an event in one place, and leaving the rest in darkness. Alfred does not occupy the centre of the illuminated area for the Chronicler is interested in Kent, and Alfred is often somewhere else—in west Wessex, perhaps, defending Exeter. Asser's *Life*, frustratingly, ends just when this last great war begins.

Alfred was not ready for a campaign, and particularly a winter campaign. Perhaps Hæsten could be tamed as Guthrum, now dead, had once been tamed? The king got in touch with the Dane and persuaded him to let his two sons be baptized. Alfred stood godfather to one, and Ethelred of Mercia to the other. The king also gave Hæsten money, and in return the Viking "bound himself with oaths". At the same time Alfred contacted the Danes of Yorkshire and East Anglia who also swore to keep the peace, and the East Anglians sent half a dozen hostages for their good behaviour. All this happened some time between the Viking landings in the autumn of 892 and the following April.

Alfred had bought time, but little else. The armies continued their raiding and when the new campaigning season opened in 893, the Danes of the Danelaw broke their agreement. "The Noise of the Arrival of these so great Forces of *Danes* unties all Bonds of Faith and Obedience between those that were settled here before and Alfred their Sovereign, the Hope of Gain and Booty prevailing more with them than the Remembrance of Faith and Oath," wrote Spelman. It seemed that everywhere the frontier that Alfred had so hardly established would be overthrown now that Guthrum was dead.

The war entered its second chapter. Alfred moved rapidly east with the main Saxon army and took up a position midway between the two invading forces "so that he might reach either of them if they tried to find any open country". This must have been at some point to the west of the Weald, perhaps where Farnham is today.

Bands from the two armies then proceeded to play a deadly game of hide-and-seek in the depths of the forest. The Danes "went through the forest in bands wherever the Saxon army happened not to be . . . and almost continuously Saxon bands were seeking the Danes both by day and night," says the *Chronicle*. The picture is a graphic one, of small bodies of men—but never, the *Chronicle* emphasizes, the whole army—padding along the forest paths that wound through the Weald.

Thanks to his earlier reorganization, Alfred was able to keep a Saxon force constantly in the field. "The king," says the *Chronicle* "divided his forces into two parts, so that half were always at home and half in the field, not counting those men whose duty it was to garrison the burhs." Now these new dispositions were to be tested to the full, for soon after Easter (which fell on 15

April that year) the war entered its third phase. Tactical raids by small bodies of men gave place to strategic moves by whole armies.

Three Danish threats developed. Hæsten, having failed to link up with the southern army, shifted his men across the Thames estuary, constructed a new large encampment at Benfleet in Essex and rested there, secure within the Danish kingdom of East Anglia. Then the Danes of East Anglia and Yorkshire sent a large fleet to the Channel with the object of creating a diversion in western Wessex and keeping Alfred pinned down there. Forty ships attacked the north Devon coast, perhaps at Cynuit, or Pilton near Barnstaple, while sixty ships laid siege to Exeter. The threat could not be ignored. If the Danes took Exeter the situation would be as dangerous as in 877, and all Alfred's work would be to do again.

The third move came from the Danish Great Army based on the south Kentish coast at Appledore. Breaking out from the safety of the Weald they conducted a raid in the direction of Hampshire and Berkshire and then, instead of returning to base, swung north-east with the object of joining their friends in the camp at Benfleet. They were intercepted at Farnham by a cavalry section, commanded by Alfred's son, Edward the Elder. He forced them to turn and fight, and completely routed them. Their commander was wounded and they were forced to leave all their booty behind. They fled northwards with Edward in hot pursuit. There was no time to find a convenient ford across the Thames—the river had to be crossed wherever the two armies struck it.

The Danes plunged on to the north, Edward followed up hard, and finally, after a pursuit of 20 miles, ran the enemy to earth six miles up the River Colne where they had taken refuge on the island of Thorney, a little to the north of the modern town of Staines.

There the Saxons closely besieged the enemy, and the Danes must have felt that their position was hopeless. So far the Saxon action had proved a brilliant success, but now a fatal weakness caused victory to slip from their grasp. The Saxons had used up all their provisions and, says the *Chronicle*, "at length the army had stayed their term of service." So the local levies went off home to have a look at the crops! It was heart-breaking, but

Edward was unable with the forces left under his command to prevent the Danes breaking out and making their way to the fort at Benfleet, which they found undefended, Hæsten and his men being away on a raid.

Alfred, with the other half of the fyrd, had been marching from the west to his son's aid when the news reached him of the Danish threat to Exeter. With a heavy heart he wheeled in his tracks and hastened back the way he had just come, sending only a token force on to London.

Edward's army had gone home, Alfred's had not arrived. The king's son was apparently not one to give up easily, however. With Ethelred of Mercia he hurried back to London and got together a new force, composed of the men from the west and the London garrison of the burh. It was clear to the two leaders that the enemy must be smoked out of their nest at Benfleet. But the Saxons had never yet been successful in storming a Danish encampment. Alfred, at about Edward's present age, had been repulsed before Reading. Still, it must be attempted.

The operation was a complete success:

> The Great Army was inside. Then came the Saxons to Benfleet and put the Army to flight and stormed the encampment and took all that was within it, both property and women and children, and brought the lot to London; and all the ships they either broke in pieces, or burnt, or brought to London or Rochester. And they brought the wife of Haesten and his two sons to the king.

It was a victory, absolute and unprecedented.

A thousand years later men cutting a railway line through Essex came on a layer of charcoal in the soil—the remains of Hæsten's camp, a memorial to Edward's victory.

Alfred appears to have remained in the west country for over a year, raising the siege of Exeter and repelling Danish threats at other points. Presumably Hæsten's captive wife and children were sent to him, unless he paid an unrecorded visit to the eastern theatre of war. At all events, Alfred returned them, unharmed, to the Danish leader.

Finding on their return that the camp at Benfleet had been destroyed, Hæsten's Danes spent some weeks constructing new defences at Shoeburyness, 10 miles further east along the coast.

Then they went out on the march again. Taking care to avoid Wessex, which had proved well able to take care of itself, "both the armies went together along the Thames and great reinforcements joined them from East Anglia and from the north. Then they went along the river till they reached the Severn, and then up that river."

The size of the Danish forces suggests that this was something more than a raid, perhaps an attempt to regain control over English Mercia. Having advanced up the Severn valley the Danes encamped at Buttington, near Welshpool.

Alfred's military organization now proved its value once again. Local levies began to move in from all directions: "from every walled town east of the Parret, from every walled town north of the Thames, from every walled town east and west of Selwood, from every walled town west of the Severn"; men from East Somerset, cavalry under Æthelhelm from Wiltshire, the Mercian army under Ethelred, even "a part also of the North Welsh people"—all converged on the camp at Buttington and settled down to besiege it.

When the Danes had eaten everything, including most of their transport horses, hunger forced them to break out. There was very hard fighting, and many of the king's thegns were killed, but in the end the enemy was defeated and "a very great slaughter was made of the Danish-men". Those who survived fled back to their base in Essex. So ended the most complete trial of strength between the two armies.

Later in this eventful year, when the Saxons were busy with the harvest, the Danes launched a second attack, having first "made safe their wives and their ships and their wealth" in East Anglia. This time they rode hard, day and night, up Watling Street, the old road leading to the north-west that formed the boundary of the Danelaw. They seized the deserted city of Chester and made themselves safe behind its Roman walls. The city was impregnable:

> The fyrd was unable to overtake them from behind before they were within the fort; nevertheless they besieged the fort from the outside for about two days, and then they took all the cattle that were there, and killed all the men whom they were able to intercept outside the fort, and burnt all the corn, and with their horses

devoured all the pasture in the neighbourhood. . . . Soon after that the Great Army moved from Wirral into North Wales, for they were unable to stay where they were; this was because they had been deprived of the cattle and corn. . . .

The scorched earth policy of the Saxons forced the Danes to abandon the whole campaign. From Wales they moved back by a devious route—"so that the fyrd might not get at them"—through Yorkshire and East Anglia to Essex. There they built a new camp on Mersea Island at the mouth of the River Colne, a few miles from Colchester.

Meanwhile the southern army, repulsed by Alfred at Exeter, called in at Chichester on its way home, no doubt with the hope of recouping its losses. "And," says the Chronicler, with a touch of smugness, "the townsmen put them to flight and slew many hundreds of them and took their ships." Once again Alfred's military arrangements had proved their strength. Towns were no longer convenient depots of plunder ripe for the taking, but hornets' nests, best left alone.

It was now the late autumn of 894. The men of the Great Army suddenly abandoned their camps in south-east Essex. They towed their remaining ships up the Thames and then up the River Lea—the river that marked the boundary of the Danelaw. About 20 miles north of London they constructed a new camp. The site is not named, but it must have lain a little to the south of Ware, probably at the junction of the Rivers Lea and Stort.

In the following summer the London burh fighters attempted to drive the Danes out of this threateningly placed camp by means of a frontal attack. But they found they had bitten off rather more than they could chew. Four king's thegns were killed and this time the townsmen were forced to withdraw, defeated.

The news brought Alfred hurrying east to tackle this new Danish problem himself now that the danger to Exeter had passed. As already observed, the king's name does not figure largely in this last war. The *Anglo-Saxon Chronicle* contains a—by its standards—very long description of the fighting in the South-east, but only mentions events in the west *en passant*. It is generally assumed that the scribe was in closer touch with the South-east, since it is obvious from occasional remarks that much was happening in western Wessex, and that this accounts for the lack of

information about Alfred; but perhaps, too, the king was feeling
the strain of his hard life, and was in general content to leave
matters to his lieutenants, his son Edward and his son-in-law
Ethelred of Mercia.

Now, once more, the old genius showed itself. First things first,
the crops must be got in: "the king encamped near to the town
while the people reaped the corn so that the Danish-men might
not deprive them of the crop." When London's food-supply had
been assured, the next problem would be how to get the Danes
out of their new camp, placed much too near to the city for anyone's comfort. Protecting the harvesters was a routine operation.
While it took place Alfred went for long rides through the
countryside, studying the lie of the land with a practised eye, and
turning over in his mind possible schemes:

> Then one day the king rode up along the river and observed
> where it might be obstructed so that the Danes would be unable to
> bring out their ships.

Control the river downstream from the Viking camp—and
there was a place where Alfred felt it could easily be done—and
the Danes would be deprived at one blow of their main weapon,
their mobile striking-force, their means of retreat. The fleet
would be marooned twenty miles from its natural element!

"Then they did thus—they constructed two forts on the two
sides of the river." From these two forts the Saxons controlled the
passage of the River Lea; Henry of Huntingdon later recorded a
tradition that they divided the river's course into three channels.

> When the Saxons had just begun the work and had encamped close
> by, the Great Army perceived that they could not bring their ships
> out. Thereupon they left them and went away across country . . .
> and the men of London fetched the ships, and those that they could
> not take away they broke up, and all that were worth taking they
> brought back to London.

Once again Alfred had out-manœuvred the enemy. London
was saved.

Having abandoned their carefully prepared camp on the River
Lea the disgruntled Danes struck north-west along the borders of
the Danelaw following much the same route that they had taken

twice before. The frontier made it easy and natural to move in the direction of Shropshire and Cheshire—English areas, but well-removed from Alfred's now powerful kingdom of Wessex.

The Danish force reached Quatford, close to Bridgnorth on the Severn, "and there they erected a fort and settled down for the winter". The fyrd had ridden westwards after them, but had been unable to prevent the enemy digging themselves in.

After wintering in their camp at Quatford, the Danes apparently decided that the game was up. No doubt they had discussed their impossible situation during the long winter nights. . . . They had spent over three years in England and had nothing to show for it. They had survived some hard knocks, but whenever they had probed the Saxon defences, they had eventually been defeated. Now they were miles from their base, the enemy at their gates. . . . This was no easier than fighting the Franks or the Flemings. The farmers of the Danelaw encouraged these unsettled and unsettling men to go back to the Continent. "The Danes that remained yet unsettled being now utterly broken and beaten out of heart in all their Attempts on Land, and becoming a Pestre and Surcharge unto their own Plantations, they provide them Shipping . . ."—that is the way Spelman puts it.

And after this year there is no record in the *Chronicle* of regular fighting during the rest of Alfred's reign. But the probability is that sporadic raiding of a disturbing but not dangerous character continued, and it is fairly clear that attacks by the Danes already established in East Anglia and Yorkshire continued to harass the Channel coast of Wessex. Indeed under Alfred's son, Edward the Elder, these attacks acquired much greater importance than those of raiders from overseas. The problem was then solved, for the time being, by the conquest of the whole Danelaw.

Meanwhile Alfred's new ships, shaped neither in the Frisian manner nor in the Danish, but as it seemed to him that they might be most useful—though "what manner of Vessel they were, whether Ships or Gallies, does not fully appear, nor will I determine", says the cautious Spelman—were apparently well able to police the coasts of Wessex.

Yet the new design was apparently not entirely satisfactory. Perhaps there were teething troubles, of the sort associated with the prototype of a new airliner, or perhaps the crews, some of whom may have been Frisians, were not at home in English coastal waters. At all events, when six raiders based on the Isle of Wight threatened the south Devon coast and Alfred sent nine of the new ships to deal with them, the Danes eventually escaped "because the ships of the others (i.e. the Saxons) had grounded . . . very disadvantageously."

The *Chronicle* gives a surprisingly detailed account of this action. Two Danish ships were taken and the crew of a third so reduced in numbers that there were not enough men left to work the ship, but the other three got away, for "the tide came to the Danish ships before the Christians could push theirs off, and so they rowed out and away." Nevertheless they were so severely damaged that two were driven ashore by the weather, and their crews were hanged by Alfred at Winchester. Only one ship, "sorely wounded", limped back to East Anglia. So in the long run the Saxons had notched up another success.

"The same summer," continues the *Chronicle*, "not less than twenty ships perished, with their crews and everything else, on the south coast." The comment is ambiguous, but its tone suggests that these were Danish losses not Saxon ones.

These, though, were mere details. The real struggle had ended in 896. Perhaps it was just as well that it had done so, for during the preceding three years plague, a by-product of war, had struck England:

"The English people were far more afflicted during these three years by pestilence, falling alike on cattle and men" than by the Danes. The bishops of Rochester and Dorchester, and the ealdormen of Kent, Essex and Hampshire were among those of the country's leaders whose deaths from plague are recorded during these years.

The most important fact though, was that the second Great Army had broken up in 896 after the winter at Quatford:

> In the summer the Great Army dispersed, some to East Anglia, and others to Northumbria. And those who were moneyless got themselves ships there and sailed south over the seas to the river Seine.
> *By the mercy of God the Great Army had not altogether broken the English race.*

Alfred's last years were passed in a half-light of war and peace.

As the danger grew less immediate he was to spend more time on his chosen pursuits. Asser described how, ten years before, the pressure on Alfred's money and time had forced him to split them into two parts.

"He vowed," writes Asser, "to devote to God half his services, both day and night, and also half of all his wealth." Alfred's budget was made up as follows: his officials divided his income into two equal parts. One half was then itself sub-divided into three equal parts; one third was to pay the king's attendants, officials and soldiers, a second was to pay the men who worked for him—"men skilled in every kind of construction"—and the third was assigned for the support of foreigners who visited his court "out of every nation far and near".

The other half of Alfred's revenue was devoted to God's service, and was divided into four parts; a quarter for the poor, a quarter for the upkeep of the two monasteries, at Athelney and Shaftesbury, that he had founded, a quarter for the upkeep of the palace school for the sons of thegns, and a quarter for the use of the Church in Wessex and Mercia "and sometimes, if necessary," says Asser largely, "throughout all Britain, Gaul and Ireland".

"The King having thus honoured God with his substance, proceeds in the same measure to honour him with his Personal Service also . . ." Alfred intended to devote half his time, as he had devoted half his income, to the service of God. This included all his duties as a king, such as the administration of justice, and not only what would today be regarded as religious duties.

In connection with this division there occurs one of the best-known tales associated with Alfred. How was he to measure his time? Sundials were all right when the sun was shining, but what about the hours after nightfall, and those days when it was cloudy or raining? Alfred "after long reflection", says Asser, hit upon a solution. He ordered a supply of candles to be made of identical length (12 ins.) and weight (12 pennies). Twelve divisions were marked off on each candle and it was calculated that each candle would burn for four hours in front of the relics on the king' portable altar.

This candle-clock was not entirely satisfactory. "Sometimes the candles would not continue burning a whole day and night till the same hour that they were lighted the preceding evening' because of the draught blowing through doors and windows, chinks in the stonework, gaps between timbers, the canvas of tents. Those continual draughts—Asser's comment is a useful reminder of the extraordinary discomfort in which even kings lived in the ninth century!

The draughts must be circumvented. "And so by a useful and cunning invention, he ordered a lantern to be beautifully constructed of wood and white oxhorn, which, when skilfully planed till it is thin, is no less transparent than a vessel of glass." The problem was solved. Seven hundred years later the invention, although now old-fashioned, still impressed Sir John Spelman: "The thing being invented, and generally very useful soon grew common, and though at this day Horning Lanthorns are but of Vulgar Use and Estimation, yet was the devising of them witty, and in the Original they were the Invention of a King."

Fighting, organizing, judging, grudging every moment of time spent—it is hardly surprising that Alfred had little leisure. We know hardly anything about his everyday life. Asser speaks in one crowded paragraph of his hunting, his supervision of workers in gold and other materials, of falconers, and huntsmen, of his new buildings, and of how he would recite by heart Saxon poems "and make others learn them". The division between work and play is a modern one—these activities were Alfred's life, at once work and recreation.

Information about the king's family is equally scanty. Some of his children died young, but five survived to maturity. The eldest, the girl Æthelflæd, had married Ethelred, the ruler of English Mercia. She seems to have inherited her father's ability, and was far from being a mere pawn on the diplomatic board. "She was," as Spelman observes, "a lady of more than Feminine Spirit." After her husband's death she took the reins of government into her own hands and ruled as the "Lady of the Mercians" until her own death on 12th July 919.

Alfred's eldest son, Edward the Elder—the same who had played a large part in his father's last war—succeeded to the throne and ruled as a powerful king from 901 to 925. Another daughter, Æthelgifu, became a nun and the abbess of her father's foundation at Shaftesbury. A third daughter, Ælfthryth, married the Count of Flanders. (William the Conqueror's wife, Matilda, was descended from this marriage.) There was a fifth child, a boy called Æthelweard, born at Winchester, who died relatively young, on 16th October 922.

Asser says that Edward and Ælfthryth were educated at court and mentions specifically that the youngest son was educated with the thegns' children in the palace school. "They are all," he added admiringly, "continually in the habit of making use of books."

In the Middle Ages, where so much is unsure, one can usually be certain at least of the year in which a great man died. In Alfred's case, the mists of conjecture, as so often with this man, have obscured the certainty. In the past different authorities have given dates ranging from 899 to 901, and the thousandth anniversary of Alfred's death was in fact commemorated in 1901. Nevertheless, the balance of probability inclines very strongly in favour of the date 26th October 899, and this is the date now generally accepted. Some time in that year Alfred was at Chelsea, planning with Ethelred of Mercia and Archbishop Plegmund the rebuilding of London. This was his last-recorded activity. There is a tradition that a little while before his death Alfred had recognized his grandson Athelstan as a future king, investing him with scarlet cloak, "Saxon sword" and so on.

The *Anglo-Saxon Chronicle* records the king's death as follows:

> This year died Alfred son of Æthelwulf six nights before All-hallowmass. He was king over the whole English race, save that part which was under the dominion of the Danes; and he held the kingdom one and a half less than thirty years. And then Edward his son took the kingdom.

An eleventh-century copy of Alfred's will survives, drawn up apparently in the eighties, perhaps at the time of his daughter's wedding to Ethelred of Mercia. It is the earliest surviving will of an English king. The royal estates are divided between his two sons, his eldest daughter, his wife, and his two nephews. A kinsman, Osferth, also receives land.

The king's personal property is divided as follows: £500 to each son; £200 to his wife and to each daughter; a smaller sum is to be given to his nephews, to Osferth, to his ealdormen, to the Archbishop of Canterbury, and to three bishops. A sword goes to Ethelred of Mercia. Two hundred pounds is to be divided among the king's followers, and £200 goes to the Church, to be divided as follows: £50 to the priesthood; £50 to "God's poor servants"; £50 to poor laymen; and £50 to the church in which Alfred is buried; and naïvely—or hard-headedly?—Alfred adds: "I am not sure if there be so much money, or more, but I think it is so. If it be more, let it be shared. . . ." •

Alfred was buried in the Old Minster at Winchester, and when his wife died soon afterwards, probably in 902, she was laid beside him. In 903, when the "New Minster" which Alfred had started to build was completed, the remains of the king and queen were moved there by their son Edward the Elder. In the twelfth century a second move took place, this time to Hyde Abbey, which had been founded by Henry I just outside the city boundaries.

As things turned out, this move proved a disaster. At the time of the dissolution of the monasteries under Henry VIII Hyde Abbey was levelled to the ground. Camden, writing about fifty years later, says: "At present the bare site remains, deformed with heaps of ruins, daily dug up to burn into lime." In 1788 the area was cleared in order to provide a site for the New Gaol. In the process three stone coffins were unearthed—and broken up. It is not at all unlikely that they held the bones of Alfred the Great, of his wife, and of their son Edward the Elder! Today there is a tennis-club where Hyde Abbey once stood. There exists an ambiguous stone —*aelfred rex, DCCCLXXXI*—as with Ozymandias, "nothing beside remains".

The Man of Letters

He who would see Wisdom with his mind's eye must
climb up little by little, like a man climbing a sea-cliff with
a rope ladder, step by step; when, if ever, he comes up on
the cliff he can look out over the shore and sea below
him. . . .

Alfred's translation of St. Augustine's Soliloquies

IN the years of peace before the last war against the Danes Alfred
had been concerned, not only to strengthen the defences of
Wessex, but also to restore her civilization. As part of that policy
he had equipped himself with a brains-trust of scholars, and Asser
had helped him to become a competent Latin scholar.

About the year 890 Alfred turned to part two of his educational
programme—the translation into English of those books "which
are most necessary for all men to know". The plan itself is a remarkable one for a Saxon king to have conceived, the execution is
even more remarkable. Five basic texts were translated, four of
them in whole or in part by Alfred himself—and this during the
very years when he was conducting successfully his last war
against a Danish Great Army.

It is hardly surprising that Alfred's reputation as a scholar out-
stripped even his successful achievement. Later ages attributed all
sorts of apocryphal works to him—collections of poems and
proverbs, the whole *Anglo-Saxon Chronicle*, and so on. Modern
scholarship has whittled the number down and we are probably
somewhere near the truth if we say that Alfred encouraged the
multiplication of copies of the *Anglo-Saxon Chronicle*, and ordered an exact Anglo-Saxon translation to be made from the
Latin text of Bede's *Ecclesiastical History*. Between them these two
records contained a history of England from the time of Julius
Caesar to the "present day". They provided the Saxons with a
historical consciousness.

Werferth the Mercian, who of all his scholars had been longest associated with Alfred, translated at the king's command the *Dialogues* of St. Gregory about the year 890. There were two good reasons for choosing this work for translation. Gregory, Pope from 590 to 604, stood in a special relationship to England, having sent St. Augustine to convert the Saxons in 596. In Bede's history the English could read how Gregory had seen foreign boys for sale in the Roman market with "fair complexions, fine-cut features, and fair hair". The Pope asked where they came from, and was told that in Britain "all the people have this appearance". They are called Angles, he was told. "That is appropriate," he said, "for they have angelic faces, and it is right they should become fellow-heirs with the angels in heaven"—not *Angles* but *angels*. The full story appears below.

Quite apart from the specific English connection, Gregory's *Dialogues* was a sound choice, for it was a very popular work amongst laymen throughout the Middle Ages. "Popular" is the keyword. The book takes the form of imaginary dialogues between Gregory and his disciple Peter; these dialogues are used as the vehicle for a series of short stories describing the lives and miracles of Italian saints, and the rewards and punishments of good and bad behaviour. They provide the "entertainment" side of the medieval Church's teaching.

Asser states that Alfred commissioned the translation from Werferth, bishop of Worcester, and that it is not "word for word", but "sense for sense". Alfred attached a short preface which has been already quoted, describing the decay of learning and outlining his educational plans. Alfred continued:

"I command thee to do as I believe thou art willing, to disengage thyself from worldly matters as often as thou canst, that thou mayest apply the wisdom which God has given thee wherever thou canst [Alfred then explains that civilized peoples have always translated classics from other languages, and continues:] Therefore it seems better to me, if it seems so to you, for us also to translate some books which are most needful for all men to know. . . ." Finally, the king wrote: "I besought my trusty friends that they would set down the instruction which follows, so that, strengthened in my mind through memory and love, I may, amid the troubles of this world, sometimes think on the things of heaven."

The book is really an anthology of short stories. Consider for instance the delightful tale of the nun and the lettuce.

One morning a nun was walking in the convent garden and enjoying the sunshine when, noticing a delicious lettuce, she plucked and ate it. Unfortunately she forgot in her excitement to make the sign of the cross first. Soon afterwards she felt extremely ill. The other nuns, suspecting the devil's work, sent for help to a nearby priest, Equitius. He came, running all the way and praying hard. As he reached the nun, the devil was heard to complain bitterly from within her:

"It's not my fault! I was sitting peacefully on a lettuce and she came along and ate me!"

Nevertheless the priest drove him out, and he never came back.

The next translation undertaken was probably another of Gregory's works, his *Pastoral Care*, written about the year 590. If the *Dialogues* were designed for the ordinary layman to read or listen to, the *Pastoral Care* on the other hand was very definitely a "professional handbook", intended for the use of bishops.

The book was divided into four parts. The first analysed the motives which might lead a man to wish to be a bishop and went on to discuss the ideal bishop. Part two described the sort of life a bishop should lead, his activities, and the spiritual foundations of his beliefs and behaviour. In the third part Gregory described the bishop's flock, the different types of people with which he would have to come in contact, and the way in which he should deal with each type. The last part explains how the ideal bishop must turn his eyes inwards to his own character. He must remember his own weaknesses, and he must try to see himself as he appears in the eyes of God.

The *Pastoral Care* had been well known in England in the past. St. Augustine had brought a copy with him when he came to reconvert the island. Bede refers to it, and so does Alcuin, calling it "medicine for all the wounds of the devil" and, writing from Charles the Great's court to one of his successors in the see of York, says: "Wherever you go, let the Pastoral Book of Saint Gregory go with you."

This was the first book translated, wholly or in part, by Alfred himself, about the year 894. Alfred probably had a translation made for him, a sort of "crib", and then with its help retranslated for himself from the original Latin. He uses concrete illustrations, on the "sense for sense" principle, in a manner very typical of his manner of thought, which always tended to concretize the abstract. It is the cast of mind of a man who was capable of inventing a method of measuring time so that his own life might be accurately divided between different activities.

This manner of thought often adds to the force of the words, even when Alfred's lack of understanding alters slightly the original meaning. When a quotation from the Book of Proverbs, "As deep water, so are the words of a wise man," becomes "A very deep pool is dammed up in the wise man's mind," something has been lost, and yet a new truth is strikingly pictured.

In his book Gregory had laid down seven maxims which a bishop should strive to follow. Gregory referred to a bishop as a *rector*, ruler, and Alfred implies that a secular ruler—who is after all God's representative on earth—should, too, govern his life by them:

The ruler must keep his body free from lust;
He must be strict in the habit of self-denial;
He must be full of the delight of learning;
He must be patient in the face of tedious problems and tiresome delays, and humble in his exercise of power;
He must have sufficient spirit and confidence to support his authority;
He must be kind;
He must be zealous and severe in a righteous cause.

Gregory's words on teaching, at the end of the *Pastoral Care*, also mirrored Alfred's own thoughts.

The teacher crows like a cock in the night, and says: "Now it is time for us to awake from sleep." . . . Let the teacher shake himself till he is awake. . . . Let him beat himself with the wings of his thoughts. Then let him wake up other men to labour. . . .

The next work made available in Alfred's scheme for the re-education of Wessex was probably an English history—the only one, in fact, then in existence. Bede's *Ecclesiastical History* had been written in the kingdom of Northumbria during its Golden Age,

and completed about the year 731. It remains one of the only two
sources of information available for the Dark Ages in Britain.
Bede had, of course, written in Latin and Alfred now commissioned a translation. This translation is usually attributed, on
stylistic grounds, to bishop Werferth. On the other hand, the
bold condensation—the work has been cut down in length by
about a quarter—is probably Alfred's doing.

Bede's *History* contained all those stories of the conversion of
England that might be expected to appeal particularly to Alfred's
audience, tales such as the well-known one of Gregory the Great's
pun—"Angels, not Angles":

> In the market-place Gregory saw some boys for sale, they had
> fair complexions, sharp features, and golden hair. He asked where
> they came from. "They come from Britain, where everybody looks
> like that." Gregory asked if the inhabitants were Christians or
> heathens. "They are heathens." "Alas!" Gregory sighed, "what a
> pity that such a handsome race should be still in the Devil's power,
> and that such beautiful faces should mask such dark minds! What
> are they called?" "They are called Angles." "That is a good name for
> them, for they have angelic faces, they must become not Angles but
> Angels."

And when Gregory became Pope he sent St. Augustine to convert the English.

With the translation of Bede may be coupled the production of
the *Anglo-Saxon Chronicle*, which brought the history of England
down to Alfred's own day. It would be natural to assume that
this was commissioned by Alfred, but unfortunately there are
textual reasons for coming to the conclusion that the main text
was produced perhaps at the command of a Somerset thegn.
Certainly it was written by somebody who was particularly
interested in the south-western counties. It is fairly certain, too,
that there was a period of activity in the copying and circulation
of manuscripts of the *Chronicle* in the years after 890, and this
"rapid dissemination of the work may owe something to (Alfred's) encouragement." Further than that it is not safe to go.

Having caused to be translated a History of England, and
having perhaps encouraged the continuation of the *Chronicle*—
which was in fact kept up-to-date for about two hundred and

fifty years after Alfred's death—the king turned next to universal history and geography.

Alfred chose to translate the *Seven Books of Histories against the Pagans* of Orosius. Orosius was a Spaniard—or perhaps one should call him "an inhabitant of modern Portugal"—who had compiled his history at the request of St. Augustine, about the year 418.

St. Augustine's own great work, *The City of God*, had been written to rebut the pagan argument that the sack of Rome in 410 had been allowed by the gods because they were angry at the Roman Empire's adoption of Christianity. Similarly, Orosius writes that Augustine had asked him to compose an account "based on all the histories and annals available, of all grievous wars, foul epidemics, baneful times of famine, ghastly earthquakes, unheard-of floods, fearful conflagrations, savage blasts of lightning, storms of hail, wretched murders and crimes" in heathen times—so that men might see how much more fortunate they in fact were in the fifth century A.D.! Apart from the accessibility of Orosius' work, there was an obvious parallel with Alfred's century, when once again a faint-hearted Christian might feel that the heathen flourished like a green bay tree while the Christian suffered, which made the work peculiarly appropriate.

The *Seven Books* run from the creation of the world to the year A.D. 407, and form a universal history, with a geographical introduction. The translation, which is generally accepted as being essentially Alfred's, is not a slavish copy. Sometimes the version is "word for word", but often it is "sense for sense", in Alfred's phrase. There is extensive cutting, the two hundred chapters of the original being reduced by half, Orosius' terms are modernized and there are comments and additions made by the king himself.

Alfred's use of modern equivalents produces some interesting parallels. Thus the vestal virgins of Rome are described as "nuns", while the Amazons become "poor homeless women" (the Saxons shared the traditional German view that woman's place was in the home, cooking and raising children!), Pharaoh's chariots are "war-waggons", and when Philip of Macedon takes to the sea, the translation records that he "became a Viking". Uriah is David's "trusted thegn", and Troy becomes a "burh".

There are two additions to Orosius' geography. There is Alfred's own description of "Germany" which he understood to mean central Europe from the Rhine to the Russian Don, and from the Danube to the White Sea—a description of great value and, in its systematic account, unique in the Dark Ages.

For Alfred, as for Orosius, the world is divided into three parts: Asia, Africa, and Europe. Around these masses lies one great connected stretch of water, "the Ocean". In the north-west part of this Ocean, in the angle made by the coasts of Gaul and Spain, is Britain. The island, eight hundred miles long and two hundred miles wide, extends a long way towards the north-east. Beyond Britain is Ireland "which we call Scotland", and beyond Ireland "is that outmost land called Thule" (probably Iceland) "which is known to few because of its great distance". And beyond Thule? Darkness. Alfred's Wessex lies on the very hem of existence.

To the south of Britain are successively Gaul, Rome, the Mediterranean, and the road to India. To the east lies "Germany", the complex of states and tribes described by Alfred, fading away into the illimitable distances of the north European plain.

At this point in his translation Alfred makes the most exciting addition to Orosius, in the form of the accounts of two travellers who had made voyages of exploration to the north and east, Ohthere and Wulfstan.

Ohthere came from the north of Norway, being a great man on that part of the coast which lies opposite the Lofoten Islands. His story begins abruptly, without any preface. "Ohthere told his lord, King Alfred, that he lived northmost of all Norsemen." He went on to describe a voyage he had made north and east to the White Sea—a voyage not paralleled in English history till Tudor times, when Chancellor and Willoughby tried to find a north-east route to India and the Spice Islands.

Ohthere told how the land to the north was all waste, except in a few places where the Finns had settlements, hunting in winter and fishing in summer.

> Once he was filled with a desire to find out how far the land extended to the north, and whether anyone lived there. So he sailed due north along the coast, and all the way he had on his starboard the empty land and on the port side the open sea. After three days

he had sailed as far north as the whale-hunters ever went. And then he continued to sail north for another three days.

At that point the coast trended east, and Ohthere waited there for a west wind, and when it came sailed before it east along that land as far as he could sail in four days. Then the coastline turned south, and he had to wait for a north wind to carry him on.

Ohthere followed the coast south as far as he could sail in five days. Then he came to a great river, and there he turned about, because all that country was inhabited on the other side of the river (he had not before touched at any land that was inhabited since he left home).

One can picture Ohthere sitting in the hall at night by Alfred's side, holding in his lap a great tusk of walrus ivory, and turning and twisting it as he spoke, watched by the bearded faces of the king's thegns lit by the torch and firelight, wondering at marvels.

Ohthere had rounded the North Cape, the most northerly point of Europe, and had sailed east and south into the White Sea —the route followed by the Arctic convoys of the Second World War. The settlements he saw and avoided were probably on the River Dvina in the neighbourhood of the modern Archangel.

The Beormas (living perhaps in Karelia on the west coast of the White Sea) "told him many details about their own country and about the countries round about them, but he did not know what was true, *because he did not see it for himself*". An admirably scientific attitude, and an unusual one for those days—but what a pity Ohthere did not record the "many details"!

Othere brought back a cargo of walrus tusks and hides—the latter "very good for ship-ropes"—and made a present of some of them to Alfred.

Ohthere gives an account of two other voyages to lands already known. One was down the coast of Norway to Oslo, the other from Oslo to the Danish *entrepôt* of Hedeby in southern Denmark, by way of Jutland and the "lands in which the Angles lived before they came to this country".

Ohthere also describes his own home in northern Norway. His land, Helgeland, is long and narrow, bounded on the landward side by mountains peopled with Lapps, and they hold all the land to the north as well. Across the mountains in a south-easterly direction, around the head of the Gulf of Bothnia, are Finns.

There is a good deal of raiding backwards and forwards across the mountains between the Finns and Ohthere's men—it sounds rather like conditions on the Border between England and Scotland in Tudor times. When the Finns come raiding they make portages across the mountains, carrying with them their canoes, which are very small and light.

The Lapps, on the other hand, pay tribute to the men of Ohthere's land, a rent of animals, birds' feathers, whalebone, and rigging of whale and seal-skin. "Everyone pays according to his birth: the highest-born pay the skins of fifteen martens, five reindeer, one bearskin, ten measures of feathers, a bear or otter-skin skirt, and two ship-ropes each sixty ells long" (about two hundred feet).

Ohthere also describes something of his own life—whale-hunting and reindeer-farming. Once he and five others killed sixty whales (average length fifty ells) in two days. "He was," writes Alfred, "a very wealthy man, owning at that time six hundred reindeer" and six decoy reindeer, used as elephants are used to lure their wild cousins into captivity. "Yet he had only twenty head of cattle, twenty sheep, and twenty swine. He had very little ploughland, and that little he ploughed with horses." It was all very different from Saxon farming.

Without warning Ohthere's story ends as if a hand had been clapped over his mouth, and the next sentence starts with the words, "Wulfstan said that he sailed from Hedeby in South Denmark to Poland and Estonia in seven days—the ship running all the way under sail." There is no indication as to who Wulfstan was, but the name was a Saxon one, and he may have been an Englishman, making an exploratory trading expedition east from the normal English market in south Denmark.

Wulfstan describes the strange customs of the Estonians. In every town is a king; and there is plenty of honey and fish in the land. The kings and rich men drink fermented mare's milk (the modern *kvass*, drunk in central Asia), and the poor drink mead. There is so much mead that no ale is brewed.

> And there is a custom that when anyone dies he lies unburnt with his relations for a month or two, and the richer they are the longer they lie above ground—sometimes it is half a year. And all the while

there is drinking and sports. Then, on the day of the funeral, they divide what property is left (after paying for the drinks and games) into five or six piles, sometimes into more. Then they lay the largest part about a mile from the house, then another part a little nearer, and so on, until it is all laid out within the mile; and the smallest portion must be nearest to the house in which the dead man lies.

(The men with the swiftest horses in the surrounding countryside compete for these piles). They then all run towards the property; he who has the swiftest horse comes to the first and largest portion, and he takes the least portion who takes that which is nearest the house; and therefore swift horses are excessively dear.

After describing this economic point-to-point, Wulfstan continues:

"There is among the Estonians a tribe that can produce cold, and therefore the dead lie so long and do not putrefy; and if anyone sets two vessels full of ale or water, they contrive that one shall be frozen, be it summer or winter."

Is this magic, or is it a garbled description of icehouses, such as English country gentlemen had in the eighteenth century?

There is no means of telling, but nearly six hundred years later Phineas Fletcher, Queen Elizabeth's ambassador to Russia, confirmed part of Wulfstan's story: "In winter those who die are piled up in a hovel, like billets in a wood stack, and in the spring every man takes his dead friend, and commits him to the ground."

After concerning himself with universal history, Alfred turned to philosophy. In his last works the king was clearly translating to satisfy himself. His choice is therefore especially interesting: *The Consolations of Philosophy* by Boethius, and the *Soliloquies* of St. Augustine.

Boethius lived in Italy in the days when the Roman Empire in the west was disintegrating into a mosaic of barbarian successor-states. At first he served the greatest of the barbarians, Theodoric, but he was eventually imprisoned for political reasons and was executed in 524. His importance lies in the fact that he provided a link between Greek philosophy and the thought of the Dark Ages. For six centuries all that the west knew of Aristotle was the fragment which Boethius had had time to translate. In his own writings Boethius was regarded as a very Christian philosopher, yet the essence of his thought was Platonic rather than specifically Christian. Of this work Bertrand Russell has written: "During the two centuries before his time and the ten centuries after it, I cannot think of any European man of learning so free from super-stition and fanaticism. . . . He would have been remarkable in any age; in the age in which he lived, he is utterly amazing." This was the man to whom Alfred now turned.

William of Malmesbury—not always a reliable witness—claims that Asser made a précis of the book for Alfred's benefit. That somebody did so is not on the face of it unlikely, this only gave him a greater freedom of action. He proceeded to add to and change the original much more liberally than he had done hitherto, so that the translation becomes really a book of his own.

In the process, something is lost: "He moves . . .," says one authority, "with the awkwardness of a barbarian among the philosophical conceptions through which he has to make his way. . . . He tries to grasp the general idea by visualizing the metaphor." But if something is lost, something is also gained. When the classical Golden Age becomes "the age when no one had yet heard of any ship-army," the abstract term must have become clear to the men of his own time—and the modern reader has learnt in addition something about Alfred himself.

Boethius, in his cell, is visited by the Lady Philosophy, and a dialogue between the two follows, partly in prose and partly in verse. Boethius complains of his wretchedness, fallen from favour and awaiting execution. Philosophy replies that this must teach him how fickle and unreliable Fortune (luck) is. She goes on to explain that the only fact in which one can place trust and rest one's hopes is the Highest Good, the unmoved Mover of the universe.

That, in outline, was the book which Alfred now set himself to interpret. In it one can feel the texture of Alfred's mind most clearly. For instance, when Boethius writes of God as the *summum bonum*—the Highest Good—Alfred picks up a chance phrase and goes on to describe God as "the highest roof" protecting all and sheltering all beneath Him. Is this a barbarian misconception, or a brilliant concretization?

In another place Alfred's extended metaphor of God as th

axle-tree on which all else depends is his own—and a very powerful one:

> . . . on the axle-tree of a waggon the wheel turns, and the axle-tree stands still, and yet supports the whole waggon and regulates its progress. The wheel turns round, and the hub at the centre moves more firmly and securely than the rim does. Now the axle is as it were the Highest Good, which we call God, and the best men move nearest to God just as the hub moves nearest to the axle. . . .
>
> The most numerous class of men is nearest to the rim. . . . Though they turn all their love towards this world, they are not able to rest there, nor do they come to anything, if they are not in some measure attached to God, any more than the rim of the wheel can make any progress if it is not fastened to the spokes, and the spokes to the axle. The hub goes nearest to the axle, therefore it goes the most securely. So do the best men. In proportion as they place their love nearer to Cod, so are they more free from care. . . .

Alfred's kinsman Ethelweard, writing in the next century, says that the king's translation of Boethius "even for those who only heard it read aloud" seemed to come alive. The comment would have pleased Alfred who had, in his preface to the *Consolations*, disarmingly hoped that his readers would not blame him if they understood the book better than he did, for "every man must speak that which he speaketh, and do that which he doeth, according to the measure of his understanding and according to his leisure."

For his last translation Alfred turned to St. Augustine's *Soliloquies*. These were written about the time that Augustine was preparing for baptism in 387. He described his purpose—"I want to know God and the soul". Once again Alfred translates freely, more so than in any earlier work, and selects only those passages that appealed to him, calling his selection "Flowers Gathered". At the close of his introduction Alfred writes that the book shows how St. Augustine's "Reason answered his Mind, when his Mind doubted about anything, or wished to know anything which it could not clearly understand before."

"God I would understand, and my own soul I would know, since I love nothing but them, and yet I know not what either of them is." Some matters, though, can be known only by Faith and not by Reason—"I know who built Rome, not because I saw it myself, but because it was told me."

Once again, as in Alfred's Boethius, with its simile of the waggon-wheel, there is an emphasis on Man's almost *physical* connection with God. At one point, for instance, Alfred writes that man is held to God as a ship is held by its cable to the shore. "Fasten your mind's eye on God, as the anchor is fastened in the earth . . . the ship will remain unbroken if the cable holds."

Wisdom must be attained by little and little:

> He who would see it with his mind's eye must climb up little by little, like a man climbing a sea-cliff with a rope ladder, step by step; when, if ever, he comes up on the cliff he can look out over the shore and sea below him, and also over the land which was formerly above him.

The love of Wisdom must be as strong as physical love:

> Thou must put thy bare body towards it, if thou wilt experience it,

There are many roads to Wisdom and some seekers are nearer their goal than others:

> Consider whether any man seeketh the King's home where he himself lives, or whether everyone comes to the King by the same road? On the contrary, I suppose they come by many ways: some come from very far and their way is evil and difficult, and some have a very long but direct and good road . . . yet they all come to one lord. . . . So is it with Wisdom . . . as in every King's court, some are in the bedroom, some in the hall, some in prison; yet all live by his favour, as all men live under one sun, and by its light they see that which they see.

The ship's cable, the rope-ladder swinging on the cliff-face, the king's court as the centre of men's life—again and again Alfred throws incidental light on the picture in his own mind and on the ninth-century life around him. The most famous of these metaphors, which gives at once a description of his own method of building up knowledge and at the same time of the physical act of building in his days, lies in Alfred's preface to the *Soliloquies*. It is the most complete piece of imaginative prose that the king produced:

I gathered straight shafts, and props, and horizontal beams, and handles for each of the tools which I could work with, and curved timbers, and upright posts, and for each of the works which I could perform I chose as many of the fittest trees as I could carry away. . . . In every tree I saw something that I needed at home. Therefore I advise everyone who can, and who has many waggons, to go to the same wood where I cut the props. There let him get more for himself and load his waggons with good wood so that he may weave neat walls, erect well-made houses, and set up a good enclosure of buildings. There he may live, happy and quiet, summer and winter, *as I never yet have done*. But He who taught me, and Who sees that the wood is good may make me live more softly in my temporal hut while I am in this world, and also in the eternal home which He has promised us. . . .

Looking over the titles of the books translated or commissioned by Alfred, or compiled during his reign, one can detect a pattern. "The *Pastoral Care* of Pope Gregory was to educate the clergy in the art of shepherding their flocks, the *Dialogues* to confirm their faith with stories about miracles. The works of Orosius and of Bede were to teach Englishmen what was known about the history of the world in general, and of the golden age of Christian England in particular; and, finally, as a stimulant for the national spirit of his countrymen, the *Chronicle* was compiled to paint the past glories of the West Saxons and to tell how the kingdom had been delivered through the hard fighting of Alfred and his followers."

To these can be added, Boethius as the receptacle of Platonic philosophy and St. Augustine as that of Christian apologetics.

How far was Alfred successful in his aims? Perhaps he had not quite, as Spelman optimistically claims, "in a short time brought it to pass that Learning and Civility, which formerly had been in Contempt, became the only Thing in request and generally desired of every Man." He failed to make Old English a literary language. Latin soon replaced it as the only respectable tongue for intellectuals, though Saxon translations continued to be made— the earliest version of the *Soliloquies* is a single twelfth-century copy. The actual work of translation was a great success. A contemporary Cornish acrostic in Latin says of Alfred that he had "learnedly run through the fields of foreign lore". One point that a modern reader is inclined to overlook is the primitive machinery of the Old English language; even to use it for the construction of an elaborate sentence was in Alfred's day very much a matter of experiment.

The Alfred Legend

"Alfred in many Passages of his Life appears to have much contemplated the Life and Actions of *Solomon;"*
Sir John Spelman, 1643

L EGENDS attached themselves to Alfred slowly and inter-mittently. He never became one of the great international figures of medieval folklore, one of the Worthies of Christendom like King Arthur, or Charles the Great. The legends that are known as the Matter of Britain were moulded round the semi-mythical Arthur and his Round Table, the "Song of Roland" was written about Charles the Great, but Alfred was too local, too level-headed a man for his life to attract to itself the great issues of good and evil, of magic and mystery. There was not quite enough drama in his brief flight to Athelney, not quite sufficient tragedy or triumph in the shifting fortunes of his struggle with the Vikings.

Nevertheless, within the limits of these islands there did cohere around the name of Alfred a growing body of mental attitudes and unsubstantiated stories that justify the use of the term "the Alfred legend".

As the legend developed one can distinguish various strands that went to its making. One, that of the great law-giver and wise ruler, the "English Solomon", was in existence within a hundred years of Alfred's death. His laws are "*the* doombook" *par excellence*, he is "the wise king", the "fountain of justice". Alfred's descendant, Ethelweard, wrote of him in these terms:

> The magnanimous King Alfred, that immoveable pillar of the West Saxons, that man full of justice, bold in arms, learned in speech, imbued with divine instructions.

These characteristics were developed by twelfth-century chroniclers, men such as Florence of Worcester and Henry of

Huntingdon. The former, taking his cue from Ethelweard, described Alfred as

> famous, warlike, victorious; the diligent provider for widows and children, for orphans and the poor; the most skilful of Saxon poets, most dear to his people, affable to all, and most generous; endowed with prudence, fortitude, justice, and temperance; most patient in the infirmity from which he constantly suffered; a most discreet investigator in the execution of justice; most watchful and devout in the service of God.

While Florence has not actually invented anything, one feels that Alfred has begun to bulk a little larger than life-size.

A second strand in the legend, developing parallel in time with that of the "English Solomon", is that of the wild young king, a sort of Prince Hal, brought low by God, forced to live *incognito* with peasants, and then, when his pride has been sufficiently abased, brought to power and glory through the intercession of the saints.

There are several slightly varying versions of this common basic pattern. They all derive, in essentials, from the story of "Alfred and the Cakes". This story first appeared in print in 1574, when it was inserted in Asser's *Life*, but it can be traced back in other places with certainty to the first half of the twelfth century, and it may be earlier than this.

The story is found in certain early writings dealing with the life of St. Neot. He was a misty Cornish saint, who lived in the tenth century (when Alfred, of course, was dead and buried). He shared a chapel in Cornwall with St. Guerir. At some date between 878 and 1020 his relics were transferred from Cornwall to Huntingdonshire. It was after this translation that the Saint's name became connected with that of Alfred, and it looks suspiciously as though this connection represents a shrewd bit of advertising on behalf of the new shrine.

The story that eventually emerged was drawn partly from the *Annals of Saint Neot* (themselves based on a lost life of the Saint), partly on a twelfth-century *Life*, and partly on a twelfth-century homily on St. Neot in Old English. This last is probably the earliest source, and it is interesting to find that there is no mention in it of Alfred actually *burning* the cakes!

The earliest version is as follows. As a young king Alfred was idle and unprincipled:

> He showed the empty-headedness of youth, and when his subjects came and laid their necessities before him, and when some who were oppressed sought his aid and protection, he refused to listen to them and to redress their grievances, treating them as if they were beneath his notice. So the most blessed Saint Neot, while yet alive, who was his relation, was much dissatisfied with him and, being filled with the prophetic spirit, predicted that many hardships would arise because of this. But the king entirely rejected his prophecy, slighting this pious reproof of the man of God, though it was perfectly correct.

In the course of time the Saint died, and eventually Alfred's punishment arrived in the shape of Guthrum and his Danes. When the king heard this news, says the legend, he immediately abandoned his people, his treasure, and his treasure-chests.

> He went skulking along by hedge and lane, by wood and field, till by God's guidance he came safely to Athelney, and took refuge in a swineherd's house, and obeyed him and his evil wife quite willingly. Now it happened that one day the swineherd's wife heated her oven, and the King sat by it, warming himself at the fire, and they did not know that he was the King. Then the evil wife suddenly grew angry and, in a bad mood, said to the King: "Turn over the loaves so that they do not burn, for I see every day what a great eater you are." He obeyed the evil wife because he had to. Then the good King, with much sorrow and sighing, cried to the Lord, asking for mercy.

Having thrown himself on God's mercy, Alfred is visited by the spirit of St. Neot. The Saint comforts the king, saying: "I go before thee, follow thou after me, together with thy people." Alfred shakes off his despair and gathers his army together. A few days later at Ethandun a venerable old man in armour, with a shining face, leads "the athletes of Christ" to victory.

This was the basic story from which all later versions derived. The central episode of the cakes soon suffered two changes. The swineherd became a cowherd, and Alfred was not merely set to watch the cakes but, sitting there preoccupied, was also allowed to let them *burn*. In this version the "unhappy housewife" rushes up and turns them, crying out to the king (in Latin hexameters!):

> Canst sit and see the bread burn thus, thou sot,
> And canst not turn what thou so well lov'st hot?

In the twelfth century William of Malmesbury records a more elaborate version of Alfred's vision. In this account the king, together with his mother, is in hiding from the Danes at Glastonbury for three years. There they are visited by a mysterious stranger, with whom the king shares their last supplies of bread and wine. After eating, the stranger vanishes, and almost immediately the king's attendants return with a huge catch—three shiploads—of fish, although it is midwinter. That night the stranger reappears to Alfred in a dream and reveals himself as St. Cuthbert. He brings the promise of pardon, the hope of victory, and ". . . all Albion is given to you and your sons. . . ."

The original story has been "up-graded"—the Biblical overtones, the substitution of the national figure of St. Cuthbert for the obscure St. Neot—everything indicates this.

The story also attracted to itself some of those floating folk-tales common to so many heroes' lives, such as the visit in disguise to the enemies' camp. While at Athelney, Alfred disguises himself as a wandering minstrel and juggler. He is able to reach the innermost tent where the Danish leaders are holding their council of war. Alfred stays in the camp for several days until he is satisfied that he knows everything. Then he steals back to Athelney, gathers his own leaders and explains how they can beat the enemy. "All leapt to the task and they fell on the barbarians defeating them with great slaughter." There is not a word of truth in all this, of course; it is simply one of the typical plot-patterns that attach themselves to legendary heroes.

The late twelfth and thirteenth centuries were the great age of courtly romance. In their sphere of entertainment Alfred could not compete with King Arthur who became the fashionable hero of the upper classes. The Alfred legends, in consequence, shift to the more prosaic milieu of the monastery and the ale-house. There is a tendency to stress the good solid virtues of the man. The Saxon King became the Doctor Dale of the period. These qualities are emphasized in a rhymed history of the period:

> After many hundred winters
> Came Alfred the king,
> England's darling,
> And made the laws in English.

In a dialogue between an Owl and a Nightingale "Alfred that was wise" is cited as the apocryphal source of the proverbs which the two birds exchange. A very elaborate collection of rhymed sayings is fathered on him under the title, "The Proverbs of King Alfred".

> The shepherd of the English,
> The darling of the English . . .
> He was king and clerk,
> Full well he loved God's work;
> He was wise in his word,
> And wary in his work:
> He was the wisest man in all England.

The poem falls into three parts. In the first Alfred describes the duty of men; this is based on the king's translation of Boethius. The second part consists of a collection of proverbs—pawky peasant sayings:

> A wise child is his father's joy,
> A child is better unborn than unbeaten,
> A fool's arrow is soon shot.
> Whoever lets his wife be his master, shall
>   never be lord of his word.
> Wherever you go, say at the end,
> Let be what may be, God's will be done.

The third part claims to record Alfred's advice to his son. The king's position is clearly defined as that of a ruler under God, *and under the law*—an important feature of the medieval monarchy.

> One can be no right ruling King under Christ himself,
> Unless he have learning, know the Law,
> And understand the use of his writts,
> And be able by his own Reading to learn how to govern
> Lawfully.

Matthew Paris, a thirteenth-century monk of St. Albans, gathered all the Alfred legends into one account. Matthew was an Englishman, strongly resentful of Henry III's Poitevin favourites, and he intended that his readers should contrast Alfred and Henry. In a manuscript at Corpus Christi College, Cambridge, there is an idealized portrait of Alfred as the writer imagined him; bearded, wearing a thirteenth-century crown and holding a sceptre in his right hand. In the left hand is a scroll: *Primus in anglia regnavi solus, scilicet monarcha* (I was the first to rule supreme in England, in fact the first king).

In the next century the legends lose all touch with reality. In the *Mirror of Justices* Alfred is made to hang forty-four unjust judges on one day; in another story he is credited with the foundation of Oxford in 886; in a third he moves into fairyland.

One day the king is out hunting when he discovers an eagle's nest in the top of a high tree. In the nest is a beautiful child, dressed in a purple robe and with gold bracelets on his arms. His name is Nestingus, and he is brought back and educated at Alfred's court. What became of him nobody knows!

Matthew Paris had already seen in Alfred a national hero. The fifteenth and sixteenth centuries, with the current of national feeling running strongly, concentrated on this aspect of the Alfred legend. In 1441 Henry VI wrote to Pope Eugenius begging him to canonize "the first monarch of the famous realm of England . . . in whom the Lord hath deigned to work miracles both in his life and in his death. . . ." The Pope refused. Spelman, writing in protestant seventeenth-century England, commented sharply: ". . . questionless had the Church of *Rome* borne the same good Will toward him that they have done to others, it had not been hard for them in the Passages of his Life to have found as good a Ground for his canonization as they have had for many whom they have Sainted."

A hundred years after Henry VI's death, Queen Elizabeth's Archbishop Parker, nicely combining patriotism and archaeological fervour, produced in 1574 the first printed life of Alfred—an edition of Asser's Life, the *Annals of the Exploits of Alfred the Great*. As has been seen, Asser's *Life* is perhaps suspect, and the Archbishop did not improve matters by interpolating uncritically the St. Neot legends—this is where "Alfred and the Cakes" finally finds its resting-place—and adding a quite imaginary portrait of the king on the title-page. Nevertheless, he had made generally available the story of Alfred.

Immediately the Alfred legend took on a new dimension, that of a vehicle for propaganda. Elizabethan patriotism saw in Alfred a hero they could recognize, standing, they felt, clear of Gothic barbarism and medieval superstition. Hakluyt, in his prose epic, repeats the story of the voyage of Ohthere, ". . . made to the North-east parts beyond Norway, reported by himselfe unto Alfred the famous king of England, about the yere 890." Here was something worthy to set beside the contemporary exploits of Drake and Hawkins.

Camden, that enthusiastic Tudor amateur archaeologist, found in Alfred's reputation ammunition for the perennial war between Oxford and Cambridge. When he edited Asser he took care to interpolate a passage referring to Alfred's re-foundation of the university of Oxford, already in Alfred's day—he says—an old foundation. On St. Martin's Eve prayers were customarily offered at Oxford for all benefactors and ". . . more especially for the soul of King Alfred, the first founder of this university." (Cambridge, it must regretfully be admitted, was no more scrupulous; it was busy claiming descent from "Cantaber, an exiled Spanish prince". In fact, of course, both universities had been founded three hundred years or so after Alfred's time. There is no historical evidence for educational foundations by Alfred.)

While the archaeologists were getting to work on Asser's *Life*, the ballad-mongers were developing the story of "Alfred and the Cakes". Within four years of Parker's edition of Asser a ballad was in existence (1578) based on his account:

> The Shepherd and the King, and of Gillian, the Shepherd's Wife, with her Churlish answers; being full of mirth and merry pastime. To the tune of Flying Flame.

In this version Alfred, dressed as a beggar, goes through Somerset in search of adventure. He meets "A Shepheard swaine of lusty limbs" who challenges him to a fight. The king loses and the shepherd hires him. Gillian is not so sure:

> "Whom have you here?" quoth she;
> "A fellow I doubt will cut our throats,
> So like a knave lookes hee."

In due course the cakes put in an appearance, and begin to burn:

> "What canst thou not, thou lout," quoth she,
> "Take pains the same to turne?"

> "Thou art more quick to rake it out
>   And eat it up half dough,
>   Than thus to stay till't be enough,
>   And so thy manners show.
>   But serve me such another tricke,
>   I'll thwack thee on the snout":
>   Which made the patient king, good man,
>   Of her to stand in doubt.

However, it all ends satisfactorily. The shepherd and Gillian are not hanged as they fear they will be when they discover who their guest is. Instead, they are given a large farm. The shepherd concludes the poem:

> And in your prayse, my bag-pipe shall
>   Sound sweetly once a yeere,
>   How Alfred our renowned king
>   Most kindly hath been here.

This was the prototype of many other ballads. One, known now as "King John and the Abbot of Canterbury" started life a "King Olfrey and the Old Abbot". In Somerset the name "Alfred" is still pronounced "Olfred".

With the outbreak of the Civil War both sides appealed to th past, drawing completely unhistorical arguments from such events as the battle of Hastings and the signing of Magna Carta It is not surprising therefore to find King Alfred being pressed into the struggle on the royalist side.

In 1634 Robert Powell published *The Life of Alfred, the first Institutor of Subordinate Government*, in which he drew detailed and impossible parallels between "a Paire of Peerlesse Princes"– Alfred and Charles I. By far the best life of Alfred was written b another royalist, Sir John Spelman. Spelman probably wrote h book while he was at the royalist headquarters in Oxford durin the early days of the war. He died in the summer of 1643 of "th camp disease" (typhus), and his book remained in manuscript fo thirty years until it was published—in a Latin translation!—with comments by Obadiah Walker, a Master of University College, Oxford, who later became a Catholic. It is in this book that Alfred is for the first time referred to as "The Great".

But Alfred's life was sufficiently varied, and sufficiently vague, for it also to appeal to Roundheads as well as Cavaliers. Milton, in his *History of Britain* (derived from Geoffrey of Monmouth) calls Alfred "the mirror of Princes", and considered writing an epic or "heroical poem" on Alfred at Athelney.

By the eighteenth century Alfred had passed beyond legend and party propaganda and had become a symbol—a neutral peg on which the most diverse compositions could be hung. The stories bud and proliferate beyond description. During the century a dozen dramas and poems took him as their subject, with titles such as: *The Patriot King*; *The Battle of Edington, or British Liberty*; *Alfred, or the Magic Banner*.

Typical of these is "*Alfred: A Masque*. Represented before Their Royal Highnesses the Prince and Princess of Wales, at Cliffden, On the 1st August, 1740. . . . The Scene represents a plain, surrounded with woods. On one side, a cottage: on the other, flocks and herds in distant prospect. A Hermit's cave in full view, over hung with trees, wild and grotesque. . . ." *Wild and grotesque*—there is summed up the whole eighteenth-century approach to the Saxons.

The swineherd and his rough wife have become sympathetic Arcadian shepherds, Corin and Emma. The opening couplet sets the tone. "Gentle Emma" speaks:

> Shepherd, 'tis he. Beneath yon aged oak,
> All on the flowery turf he lays him down.

We are a world away from the original band of guerrilla fighters, up to their thighs in mud. Alfred has given up hope ("O despair! O grief of griefs!"). New heart is put into him by the Earl of Devon—no nonsense about saints for the eighteenth century ("Be of comfort: we can but die at last"), and by the Gothic hermit ("Attach thee firmly to the virtuous deeds and offices of life"). Additional moral support is rapidly provided by his Queen, Elfrida ("My lord, my life, my Alfred!"), by the spirits of Edward III, *his* Queen Philippa, and their son the Black Prince; by

"The great Eliza" (Elizabeth I); and finally by William III, "Immortal William", from whose accession

> Shall *Britain* date her rights and laws restor'd:
> And one high purpose rule her sovereign's heart;

Opposed by such cheer-leaders, it is clear that the Danes will never have a chance. As a climax, the Saxon army listen to a venerable Bard, who sings an Ode, which turns out, amazingly, to be—"Rule Britannia"!

The Hermit concludes the entertainment with a speech on the advantages of sea-power;

> *Britons*, proceed, the subject Deep command,
> Awe with your navies every hostile land.
> In vain their threats, their armies all in vain:
> They rule the balanc'd world, who rule the main.

The play was published within three weeks, and later revived as an opera, first performed in Dublin in 1745. "Rule Britannia", the words of which were probably by James Thompson, rapidly became popular.

The rational nature of Alfred's achievements exerted an understandable fascination on eighteenth-century minds. Dr. Johnson pondered the idea of composing a life of Alfred; Hume, in his History, wrote, "He seems, indeed, to be the model of that perfect character which, under the domination of a sage or wise man, philosophers have been fond of delineating, rather as a fiction of their imagination than in hopes of ever seeing it really existing."

The Romantics, in their turn, were just as responsive. Blake, Keats, Shelley and Wordsworth all found it natural to refer enthusiastically to Alfred.

In 1798 the king was the subject of a ballet performed at Sadler's Wells.

The year 1801, the presumed anniversary of Alfred's death saw the erection of the monument at Athelney:

> King Ælfred the Great, in the year of Our Lord 879, having been defeated by the Danes, fled for refuge to the forest of Athelney where he lay concealed from his enemies for the space of a whole year. He soon after regained possession of the throne; and in grateful remembrance of the protection he had received, under the favour of

Heaven, he erected a monastery on this spot, and endowed it with all the lands contained in the Isle of Athelney. To perpetuate the memory of so remarkable an incident in the life of that illustrious prince, this edifice was founded by John Slade, Esq., of Maunsel, the proprietor of Athelney, and lord of the manor of North Petherton, A.D. 1801.

In the thirties there was even a weekly paper *The Alfred, London Weekly Journal, and Bridgwater and Somersetshire General Advertiser.*

There were celebrations on a Victorian scale of the millennial anniversaries of Alfred's birth (1849) and death (1901)—medals, speeches, subscriptions, collected editions of the king's works, and so on. A battleship, the *King Alfred*, was launched, and an ubiquitous daffodil named after him.

It was in 1901 that the statue at Winchester was erected, the work of Hamo Thornycroft. Scabbarded sword held aloft in the sign of the Cross, the statue, which with its plinth stands about 24 feet high, looks strongly west, and seems to have a certain dignity denied to the figure at Wantage. The single word "Ælfred" is carved on the base at the front. Beneath it is the information:

> To the Founder of the kingdom and nation
> D. October DCCCCI
> Winchester and the English Name
> September MDCCCCI

> Earl of Rosebery   — Orator
> Hamo Thornycroft — Sculptor
> Alfred Bowker   — Mayor

From the rear emerge two small, mysterious lead pipes. Across the road to the right, the King Alfred Motor Services, to the left, the public lavatories.

In that year of Queen Victoria's death, the place of Alfred was clear. It is described unambiguously in a little blue-backed paper pamphlet ("An edition can also be had in Cream Cloth at Three Shillings net") by J.A. H-S.

"Comparison," he writes, "we know is in some instances, obviously odious; yet, with an eye upon the ENGLAND of

ALFRED'S age, and one upon the VICTORIAN age, just closed, there are many and numerous points in common. To sum up all— *the one is but the fulfilment of the other.*"

If the king and queen could have met, which of them, one wonders, would have been the more astonished at this remarkable conclusion?

During the nineteenth century, too, the fictional mining of the Alfred legend had continued. Thomas Hughes, in *Tom Brown's Schooldays* (1857), takes the high and patriotic line:

> . . . now we leave the camp, and descend towards the west, and are on Ash-down. We are treading on heroes. It is sacred ground for Englishmen, more sacred than all but one or two fields where their bones lie whitening. For this is the actual place where our Alfred won his great battle, the battle of Ash-down ('Æscendun' in the chroniclers) which broke the Danish power, and made England a Christian land.

Thackeray, as one might expect, takes a more sophisticated look at the Victorian attitude to Alfred in *The Newcomes* (1854). Mr. Gandish of Soho is showing Colonel Newcome some pictures:

> You know the anecdote, Colonel? King Alfred, flying from the Danes, took refuge in a neat'erd's 'ut. The rustic's wife told him to bake a cake, and the fugitive sovering set down to his ignoble task, and forgetting it in the cares of state, let the cake burn, on which the woman struck him. The moment chose is when she is lifting her 'and to deliver the blow. The king receives it with majesty mingled with meekness. In the background the door of the 'ut is open, letting in the royal officers to announce the Danes are defeated. The daylight breaks in at the aperture, signifying the dawning of 'Ope.

Victorian burlesque claimed Alfred too. Consider, for example:

Alfred the Great,
The Inventive King.
An Historical Comic Opera in Three Acts
Originally written and composed for the Dome Entertainment
of the Brighton Grammar School.

Here Gilbert-and-Sullivan derivatives mingle with patriotism and pantomime in a fascinating mish-mash. The "Suggestions" at the beginning set the tone nicely: "the cheap Prussian helmets on sale at the toy-shops will serve as a basis for headgear . . . Carefully got-up Danes will be an immense success. . . ." In the ladies' dresses "a good deal of latitude may be allowed, and probably a Grecian style will prove as good as anything . . . the scenes should be very pretty."

At a banquet of Saxons the chorus greet Alfred as follows:

> He has made with the aid, at least, of a priest
> Many books in our native vernacular;
> And the trips of his ships in a host near the coast
> Give effects that are highly spectacular.
>
> > etc.

Alfred replies:

> Thank you, but you have anticipated some of my inventions. Still, I intend to make them, so there is no great harm done. . . . If you know anything of the theory of evolution, you will understand how they must develop in ages to come. Instead of using lantern-clocks, people will carry the time in their waistcoat pockets (*sensation*), and the Waterbury watch will be a household word. You would hardly understand what I meant if I were to talk to you of the future discovery of the phonograph, the telephone, and of Beecham's Soap.

And so on.

The cakes are duly burnt (*Alfred:* "I am *so* sorry, but don't you think 'The Lost Cakes' would make a fetching title for a song?"), the Danes defeated, and at the grand finale they all join hands and sing:

> Peace and plenty now shall reign,
> Saxon joining hands with Dane.
> Surely that should be the case;
> We are both of northern race.
> All our fathers vikings bold,
> Cast in an heroic mould.
> Stand we bravely back to back,
> 'Neath the glorious Union Jack.

With the opening of the twentieth century Alfred's reputation suffered something of an eclipse. The first signs of this are perhaps to be found in the review by Geoffrey Cotterell of a poem by the laureate, Alfred Austin, with the title *England's Darling*. Writing in 1896, Cotterell says of Alfred, or at least of Alfred's character as interpreted by the Victorians: "He is too much of a paragon, too blameless, too unerring, too remote."

If this feeling was beginning to creep in at the time of the Diamond Jubilee, it became increasingly general during the first half of the twentieth century. The "de-bunking" type of biography made fashionable by Lytton Strachey found its subjects in later centuries. The nine hundredth anniversary of Alfred's birth passed comparatively unnoticed.

Alfred the Great

"To be short, the prince is the life, the head and authority
all things that be done in the realm of England."
                                        Sir Thomas Smith, 1565

IT is important that a country should, in each generation, re-assess its great men. New evidence has not always been brought to light, but new scales of values have always come into use as measuring-rods.

When, attempting to assess Alfred's achievement, one regards the information available, certain, uncertain, and legendary, one thing becomes clear—the difficulty in striking a clear balance. There is an elusive, Kafkaesque quality about so much of the evidence. Again and again one is presented with an apparently solid fact and then, when one reaches out to grasp it, the evidence proves impalpable. Certainties show a disconcerting ability to become uncertainties. Consider the written evidence. The relevant entries in the *Anglo-Saxon Chronicle* would cover perhaps sixteen printed pages. Invaluable, but meagre. Asser's *Life*—the earliest manuscript was destroyed by fire in 1731, and it is at least possible that the whole thing was written a hundred and fifty years after the events it sets out to describe.

Later chroniclers misinterpreted their sources. Thus Gaimar, reading in the *Anglo-Saxon Chronicle*: "there came a great summer-fleet (sumar-litha) to Reading", records: "Then there came a Danish tyrant, Sumerled the Great", and adds mysteriously, "but he died; he lies in a closed place"! Consider the material evidence: we do not know with certainty the site of Alfred's victories; the baptism of Guthrum—it certainly took place at Aller, but where was that? For there are two possible sites, a dozen miles apart.

We do not know what Alfred looked like—the conventional heads on his coins suggest a heavy-featured, beardless man—but this type of portrait was often no more than a conventional diagram. The bones of his ancestors were jumbled like jigsaw pieces. The site of his own tomb was wrecked, disregarded, and ultimately levelled to make room for a gaol. Even the date of his death is a matter for controversy. In English history no figure of comparable stature since Alfred's day presents so many unsolved, and probably insoluble, problems.

And yet. . . .

And yet, there are certainties. The first and most striking is the way in which, from within a generation or so of his death until the present day, men have agreed that this man was great. The testimonials start with Ethelweard, in the tenth century:

> . . . that immoveable pillar of the West Saxons, that man full of justice, bold in arms, learned in speech, and, above all things, imbued with divine instructions. For he had translated into his own language, out of Latin, unnumbered volumes. . . .

Seven hundred years later the Cavalier, Sir John Spelman, writes:

> . . . the King was ever exercising of himself, he became a Man beyond the Hopes of any Emulation, having (with a threefold Conquest) in his Enemy got the Mastery of War, in his people of Vice, and in his own Person of human Frailty; so that becoming now a Light of more than ordinary Splendour, and placed upon so eminent a Candlestick as a Throne is, there was no Place in Christendom that received not the Glory of his Beams.

For Gibbon, that eighteenth-century admirer of Marcus Aurelius, he is ". . . the greatest of English kings". The very different nineteenth-century historian, Bishop Stubbs, sees in Alfred one of the five "conscious creators of English greatness". Sir Frank Stenton, the twentieth-century authority on the period, writes that the king was:

> . . . the most effective ruler who had appeared in western Europe since the death of Charlemagne . . . beneath his preoccupation with duties, often of desperate urgency, there was always a sense of imponderable values.

Peter Hunter Blair, in one of the most recent studies of Anglo-Saxon society, concludes:

Either of his two great achievements, the military or the literary, would by itself have been sufficient justification for the verdict which posterity has passed on this remarkable man.

On what then is this unanimity of opinion, existing over so many centuries and expressed by men so different in character and outlook, based? Blair makes the point most clearly: Alfred's military successes against the Danes, and his intellectual triumphs over ignorance and barbarism. To which one might add a third quality, his versatility. This would be surprising in any period, for the conquerors are seldom Solomons, and the scholar-kings too often lose their battles, but it is doubly remarkable in the ninth century when an infant civilization was apparently dying from internal confusion and external threats.

It is this versatility, rather than originality in the strict sense of that word, which strikes one. Alfred was constructive, rather than inventive. Wessex was the one kingdom, and Alfred the one man in England, able successfully to resist the Vikings. Without that successful resistance it is as certain as anything can be in history that Scandinavian rulers would have established themselves throughout the British Isles and the whole of our subsequent history would have taken a different pattern. For Alfred the defeat of the Danes was an exercise in the practical application of fresh techniques: the new ships, the burhs, the rota system in the fyrd may all have been adapted after a good hard look at what was happening in Europe. But if the methods were not original, nevertheless the achievement remained. It was Alfred who saw what needed to be done, and it was Alfred who provided, particularly in the dark days of 871 and 878, the will to win. So, at the close of his reign, his chronicler could modestly claim "By the mercy of God the Great Army had not utterly broken the English race." One notices that he wrote "the English race" and not just "the men of Wessex". That, too, was Alfred's doing.

Within the limits of his age Alfred's cast of thought was scientific. Always within those limits, of course—for him the earth is still fixed, firm and upright, at the centre of the spinning heavens. "Almighty God has so created all his creatures that each is in conflict with the other, so that they may not break away, but are brought round to their old route and start afresh. . . . While the creatures obey, their Creator sits on His throne and guides them all." The river, Alfred writes, runs into the sea, from the sea the water sinks into the earth and works its way back till it reaches *the very spring* from which it set out. The universe dances in an ordered pattern, arranged by God.

It is not, obviously, in this that Alfred is ahead of his days—but in his reception of new ideas. With these, too, he is willing to experiment and to adapt.

> We may . . . see the King's Genius in the true Nature, no soft or roaring Melancholy, feeding itself with a superficial Running over all Variety of Objects, but advised and industrious, to choose and pursue such only as he might best convert into either publick or private Benefit.

And, above all, he wants to understand the *explanation* of everything. He sits and listens with equal attention to Ohthere speaking of Lapland, and to Asser speaking of Latin grammar.

It is in the translations that sprang, directly or indirectly, from those readings in Latin that one approaches closest to the mind of the man. Indeed, in their turns of phrase and in their interpolations, the king's writings provide a direct contact with Alfred which compensates for much of the mistiness already referred to. Alfred is perhaps the only Englishman before the Conquest—certainly the only English layman—the pattern of whose thought we can know with some certainty.

What sort of man emerges? One with an inquisitive, inquiring, intelligent, *well-balanced* mind. Above all, a religious man. It has been argued that Asser (or whoever wrote "Asser") over-emphasizes the religious aspect, so that Alfred becomes "almost a crowned monk". But this, one feels, is to under-emphasize the religiosity of the age. It was a time (as has been recognized by the same writer) when "battles began with a Mass, wars ended with a baptism". And in Alfred's writings the religious outlook forms a constant ground bass accompaniment:

> Wisdom is of such a nature, that no man in this world can comprehend her as she really is. Nevertheless everyone strives to the full extent of his understanding, to understand her if he may. But Wisdom is able to understand us completely. For Wisdom is God.

Those words from Alfred's translation of Boethius give the essence of the matter.

From hints in other places one can construct some other facets of his philosophy. Friendship is most valuable:

> For of everything else man is desirous in order that he may obtain something else through its possession; but from his friend he expects nothing but friendship and fidelity.

The continuous practice of charity is important: Alfred repeats with approval Titus' saying, "I count a day lost on which I do not do any good." The good deed must in the end be successful, if not in this world, then in the next; "Though the good may not perfect their work, yet they have an unwavering purpose, and this sincere will is itself to be reckoned a perfect work." And this from a barbarian ruler of a corner of a barbarian island, long-haired, cross-gartered, kilted and cloaked like an eighteenth-century Highlander!

Yet the intellectual achievement must be balanced against the royal strength. One is brought back again and again to the hard fact of the barbarian king who *was* a king, who tamed the Vikings and who—as Spelman emphasizes, when he links Alfred with Charles I, speaking of the latter as "the Lineal Heir and Successor of him that was the first Imperial Founder of *English* Monarchy"—was "a most Absolute Monarch. Yet", Spelman continues, "when we speak of *Alfred's* Absoluteness, it must always be understood of such a Kind of Absoluteness and Sovereignty as was agreeable to the Condition of those Warlike Times."

It must indeed, for Alfred was at the same time "a most Absolute Monarch" and a limited monarch. His laws and his example to his successors kept alive the king's legislative powers in England at a time when those powers were atrophying in other west European kingdoms. But the law in its turn made the king. "There may no right king be," says the apocryphal Proverbs of Alfred, "unless he have learning, *and know the law.*"

Alfred gave the monarchy of Wessex the prestige and power necessary for its development into the kingdom of England. Royalty had been ". . . ambulatory among the several Princes of the Heptarchy . . . feeble and of small Regard" until Alfred began "to draw the Traces of a Monarchical Platform. . . ."

The king is absolute within the law, but his authority depends for its efficiency on the co-operation of all classes, on the reliability of the tools with which he works at his craft of kingship. As Alfred writes in the great seventeenth chapter of his translation of Boethius:

> . . . no man can show any skill, or exercise or control any power, without tools and materials . . . These are a king's materials, and the tools with which he governs: a land well-peopled with men of prayer, men of war, and men of work. Without these tools no king can do his work. Beside the tools he must have materials: that is, provision for the three classes, land to live on, gifts, weapons, meat, and ale, and clothes, and whatsoever else they need. Without these the king cannot preserve the tools, and without the tools he cannot accomplish anything that he ought to do.
>
> Therefore I desired these materials by which to exercise my power, that my talents and fame should not be forgotten and concealed. But every craft and every power soon becomes old, and is passed over in silence if it be without wisdom.

There is Alfred's *credo*, what the seventeenth century would have called his political testament. He concludes:

> Whatsoever is done foolishly can never be considered as skilful. This must now above all things be said: that I wished to live honourably and after my life to leave to the men who came after me my memory in good works.

It is a good epitaph for Alfred the Great, and beside it may be set a saying of his old enemies, the Vikings:

> One thing will never die, the reputation we each leave behind at our death.

Main Sources

Original Sources:

The Anglo-Saxon Chronicle, ed. D. Whitelock, London, 1961
Asser's Life of King Alfred, ed. W. H. Stevenson, Oxford, 1959
English Historical Documents, vol. I, *c.* A.D. 500–1042, ed.
  D. Whitelock, London, 1955

Later Lives of Alfred:

The Life of Alfred the Great, Sir John Spelman, Kt. (ed.
  T. Hearne), Oxford, 1709
Alfred the Great, B. A. Lees, New York, 1915
Alfred the Great and his England, E. S. Duckett, London, 1957

General Histories:

The Beginnings of English Society, D. Whitelock, Penguin
  Books, London, 1952
The Vikings, J. Brøndsted, Penguin Books, London, 1960
An Introduction to Anglo-Saxon England, P. H. Blair, Cam-
  bridge, 1956
Anglo-Saxon England and the Norman Conquest, H. R. Loyn,
  London, 1962
A History of the Anglo-Saxons, vol. II, R. H. Hodgkin, Oxford,
  1953
Anglo-Saxon England, Sir Frank Stenton, Oxford, 1947

On the sites of Alfred's battles of Ashdown and Ethandun:

Battlefields of England, A. H. Burne, London, 1950
More Battlefields of England, A. H. Burne, London, 1952

Index